The Organization and Architecture of Innovation

Managing the Flow of Technology

The Organization and Architecture of Innovation

of Innovation

Managing the Flow of Technology

THOMAS J. ALLEN
Massachusetts Institute of Technology • Cambridge, Massachusetts, USA

GUNTER W. HENN
Henn Architekten • Munich and Berlin, Germany

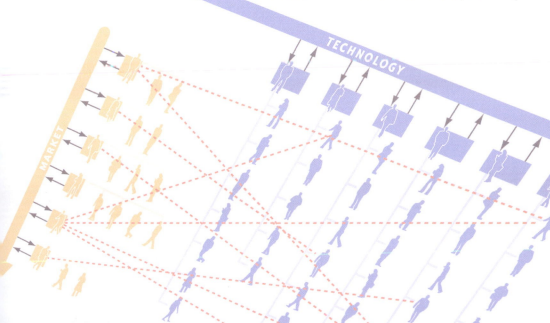

AMSTERDAM • BOSTON • HEIDELBERG • LONDON
NEW YORK • OXFORD • PARIS • SAN DIEGO
SAN FRANCISCO • SINGAPORE • SYDNEY • TOKYO

Butterworth-Heinemann and Architectural Press are imprints of Elsevier

ELSEVIER

First Published by Butterworth-Heinemann
This edition published 2011 by Spon Press
2 Park Square, Milton Park, Abingdon, Oxon OX14 4RN

Simultaneously published in the USA and Canada
by Taylor & Francis Group, 711 Third Avenue, New York, NY 10017, USA

Library of Congress Cataloging-in-Publication Data

Application submitted

British Library Cataloguing-in-Publication Data

A catalogue record for this book is available from the British Library.

ISBN 13: 978-0-7506-8236-1
ISBN 10: 0-7506-8236-1

Contents

v

Acknowledgments

WE MUST CONFESS AT THE OUTSET that listing only the names of two authors on the cover is unfair. To produce a book of this nature requires many collaborators and a few "tolerators" as well. Among the principal tolerators are the families of the two authors, especially Tom Allen's wife, Joan, who put up with the many long hours of work that were required to analyze the data upon which much of the book is based. Also among the tolerators are Allen's and Henn's students, who often had to tolerate a distracted teacher or advisor and who were very kind in not complaining. Finally, there are Allen's grandchildren, who don't realize it but who missed out on the greater attention they might have received from their "Pop."

The collaborators are even more numerous. The management of the many companies from which data were collected, especially BMW, Skoda, and Steelcase. Special thanks go to Jost Schulte-Wrede and Gerald Weber for their help and support and especially their thoughts throughout the project. We also owe thanks to the management of the Skoda assembly plant where we conducted interviews and to the faculty of the Technical University of Munich. At MIT, deep thanks go to colleagues (the four "old warhorses") Ralph Katz, Ed Roberts, Jim Utterback, and Eric von Hippel, whose help and support have had a powerful impact on Tom Allen's thinking over the years, as well as to the support staff, especially Kathleen Connolly, who worked on innumerable early chapter drafts, many of which arrived on her desk by fax from Ireland. Then there are the dozens of MIT graduate students who gathered and analyzed the data upon which so much of the book is based. They deserve our special gratitude. The software used in analyzing the network data was developed by Varghese George and an army of MIT undergraduate students, along with Jake Wetzel, another graduate student. In Ireland, we had much needed help from Ann Naughton, who provided, in addition to logistics, greatly valued and appreciated psychological support and encouragement, and from Liz Knight and Gillian Brown, who always managed to find space for our many meetings.

The design studio of Henn Architekten worked with great enthusiasm to transform organizational considerations into physical space. Especially deserving of mention are Gerhard Ziriakus for the Skoda factory, Joachim Bath for the Technical University of Munich, and Christian Bechtle for the BMW Projekthaus.

Finally, there was the indomitable team of Christine Kohlert and Scott Cooper, without whom this book would have never happened. Christine is an architect and assistant at the Technical University in Dresden. She coordinated the meetings between the authors, prepared the illustrations, and worked on the text. Scott is a professional writer and is truly professional in the best meaning of that term. His understanding of both German and English made the task so much easier and actually enjoyable. This included even a last-minute reshuffling of the chapters, which he handled with aplomb.

THOMAS J. ALLEN
GUNTER W. HENN
CAMBRIDGE, MASSACHUSETTS, MARCH 2006

About the Authors

THOMAS J. ALLEN is Howard W. Johnson Professor of Management at the Sloan School of Management, Massachusetts Institute of Technology and Professor of Engineering Systems in MIT's Systems Engineering Division. He is currently Co-Director of the Leaders for Manufacturing and Systems Design and Management Programs at MIT.

Specializing in technology and innovation management, Tom Allen explores the relationship between organizational structure and behavior. He discovered the role of technological gatekeepers in technology transfer, and has been able to quantify how a building's layout influences communication. He is also an expert on international technology transfer, reward systems for technical professionals, and how organizational structure affects project performance. He has been engaged in long-term research on project management in several industries.

Prof. Allen's first book, *Managing the Flow of Technology* (MIT Press, 1984), is the pioneering work in how people in technical organizations communicate. His work is widely cited in both the academic and general literature.

OLIVER SOULAS

GUNTER HENN, a noted German architect, established his firm HENN Architekten in 1978. The firm is based in Munich and has an office in Berlin. Gunter Henn is a Professor of Architecture at the Technical University of Dresden and a Visiting Professor at the MIT Sloan School of Management. His innovative building designs include, among many others, the BMW Research and Innovation Centre in Munich, Volkswagen's Automobile City in Wolfsburg, the celebrated Transparent Factory in Dresden, a novel auto assembly plant for Skoda in the Czech Republic, and the Faculty for Mechanical Engineering at the Technical University of Munich. He is the author, with D. Meyhöfer, of *Architektur des Wissens / Architecture of Knowledge* (Junius Verlag, 2003).

Introduction

THE REALIZATION THAT physical space and organizational structure interact to influence organizational communication patterns is what brought two such different authors together. One is a former product development engineer who became a social psychologist to study the phenomenon of technical communication. For several decades, his primary research interest has been the way people in technology-based organizations communicate. Over time, that interest blossomed to encompass what it is about communication that strengthens or hurts an organization, and the role of communication in the innovation process. The other author is a practicing architect who became interested in this topic because so many clients came to him asking how to improve communication among scientists and engineers in their organizations. Although these clients thought a spatial solution was needed, it soon became apparent that an organizational solution was needed as well.

Together, we have exchanged ideas and worked together on problems for some 20 years; *The Organization and Architecture of Innovation* is the result of that collaboration.

1

In the chapters that follow, you will see how the ideas and concepts that flow from the research of one author have been creatively transformed by the other author in spatial concepts that later can be seen physically in the steel, glass, and concrete of beautiful and functionally effective buildings. These buildings include laboratories, research and development centers, a technical university, and assembly plants. With the design of each building, the challenge was to create a space that allowed for optimal communication. The collaboration enabled the architect to see that his designs could do more than house organizations, but also provide the physical space within which certain types of communication—and hence innovation—could flourish.

Our book speaks of communication, knowledge, and innovation. Our discussion and suggestions are based on two main premises. One straightforward premise is that if you maximize the *potential* that people in an organization can and will communicate (not the amount of communication, but the potential), you will vastly increase the likelihood of knowledge transfer, inspiration, and hence innovation. The second premise is somewhat more complicated and has to do with the ways in which maximizing that potential takes place.

The traditional focus has been almost exclusively on how people are organized into groups, departments, project teams, and so on. We show, however, that organizational structure is only part of the equation. There are two tools: organizational structure *and* physical space, which can—and must—be configured to encourage the very communication that *spurs* innovation. For a given organization, this could mean starting from scratch with the way physical space is used, and seeing its relationship to organizational structure in a completely new way. The success of the innovation process today depends on the employment of both tools.

At the heart of our argument is the concept of *awareness*, in all its many facets and permutations. The awareness of which we speak throughout this book is not the kind you might experience standing alone in an art museum, where the space has been created to make you aware of the beauty the artists have created. We are concerned with awareness that does not play out for you alone. Awareness within organizations is the result of a communication process that involves many people. It is critical to innovation, and it is always a spatial phenomenon.

Why "spatial"? Because we are spatial and in time, we see people with whom we work in a space. We meet people and discuss ideas in a space. We are aware of the work of others primarily by seeing it. We cannot be aware without being in space.

Architecture figures in this book, but this is not a typical book about architecture. Most people are accustomed to considering architecture from the aesthetic viewpoint. They see a building as an object that can be spoken about largely in terms of what it looks like and, to a lesser degree, how the building "works" for those who use it. Here, in this book, architecture is not only an aesthetic discipline but rather the execution of the ideas embodied in using the two management tools of organizational structure and physical space. Architecture here does not simply structure the spaces in which we live, work, and move, but also plays a role in how we live, work, and move in those spaces. The reason is that the configuration of space can initiate and influence social behavior.

The business organizations we describe in this book are social organizations and, as such, have both an organizational dimension and a spatial dimension. The complexities of the innovation process, we contend, requires that they recognize that these two dimensions are linked intimately, and hence that businesses must respond accordingly.

Space and Social Behavior in Organizations

Architecture is a social fact that forms spatially. A simple example illustrates how space and organization fit together. In Figure I-1, we see the cloister and cell of a typical monastery. In the monastery, space has been configured so that the cell gives he who occupies it room for *concentration* on the individual level and the cloister allows for *communication* on the group level (Figure I-2). Thus, the monastery reflects two spatial elements of social behavior.

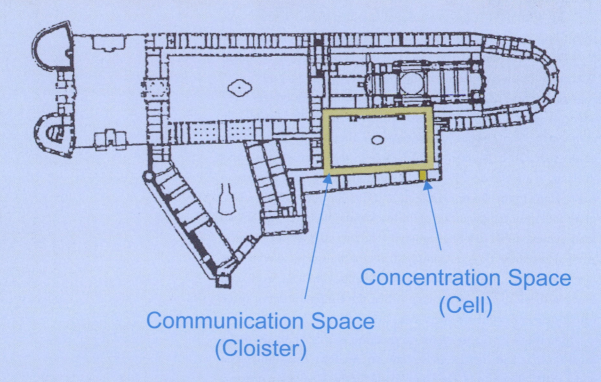

Concentration Space
(Cell)

Communication Space
(Cloister)

Figure I-1 The layout for a cloister shows that the idea of providing spaces in a building for both concentration and communication is not something new, but was recognized many years ago.

Figure I-2 Concentration and Communication

Chapter 1 introduces the innovation process and—through some relatively simple examples—begins to show the role physical space plays in the process of communication, which is vital to the innovation process.

In Chapter 2, we expand the discussion of the innovation process, particularly in the context of three types of communications in technical organizations. We trace the evolution of how organizational structure has been used to plan and manage innovation. This evolution reached an impasse as the limitations of the so-called "matrix organization" were reached. We argue that this is the point at which the issue of physical space becomes an equal partner with organizational structure as two management tools. We make this point with our Trumpet model of the product development process.

Chapter 3 links organizational structure and physical space together more tightly, and explores how communication flows in space in communication networks. We show some examples of how physical space configuration can help or hinder the necessary flow of communication, and we detail two building examples where specific consideration was given to space configuration in the context of organizational structure. These early examples set the stage for the more deliberate architecture presented in the final two chapters.

Chapter 4 returns to awareness, detailing why it has become key in the innovation process. This chapter also has extended discussions of two buildings conceived and created by one of the authors in which the principles developed in earlier chapters were applied to physical space configuration.

Finally, in Chapter 5, we show the culmination of all the principles espoused in this book. In BMW's Projekthaus in Munich, we see the unification of two management tools, organizational structure and physical space, in a building especially created to house a company's innovation workers. From this example, we draw some lessons and present some concluding thoughts.

Organization and Architecture

THIS BOOK IS ABOUT INNOVATION and the innovation process, particularly the development of innovative new products. What is innovation? Many decades ago, Joseph Schumpeter offered a now-classic definition of an innovation as something new or improved. Specifically, he defined innovation as the new combination of productive means as follows: (1) the introduction of a new good—that is, one with which consumers are not yet familiar— or a new quality of a good; (2) the introduction of a new method of production; (3) the opening of a new market; (4) the conquest of a new source or supply of raw materials or half-manufactured goods; or (5) the new organization of any industry (Schumpeter 1934).

A far simpler definition is offered by Stephan Schrader (1996). He defines the term by drawing the distinction between an invention and an innovation. Taking off from this, imagine a picture of a small town somewhere in the Wild West of America in the mid-nineteenth century. In the center is a railroad, Schrader's example of *the* invention of the time. But it is only an invention. Taking the analogy further, he argues that we don't know where the railroad goes. We can only guess at the unknown region to which it might travel. It is an invention that represents some technical progress, but it is not in and of itself an innovation.

In 1883, the director of the U.S. Patent Office declared that the office "may well be closed since all the important discoveries have been made." He, too, spoke of inventions, not innovations, but Schrader uses this to get us closer to a definition of innovation.

> This was a small error, because a few years later, in Europe, a patent was filed for an invention that has probably had an impact unlike any other in our lifetime: the automotive engine.
>
> But just as the director of the U.S. patent office had erred, so too did Carl Benz and Gottlieb Daimler underestimate their invention. They assumed that the motorcoach would replace the horse-drawn carriage. But they never assumed that the automobile would transform our way of life. (Schrader, 1996, p. 5)

Benz and Daimler failed to realize the impact of the motorcoach because they thought about it only as an invention, not as an innovation. It is an important distinction because it speaks directly to the question of whether the innovation *process* can be planned—a central aspect of our discussion in this book.

> Innovation is invention and application. Or, put differently: innovation is invention and exploitation. Thus we come to the question posed: can innovation be planned?… Planning now refers to two dimensions. The first is the dimension of the invention. Can one plan an invention? Can one predict the directions in which scientific knowledge and technical progress will develop? Second is the application of the invention. Can one predict the purposes for which an invention can be used and how the invention will become important?…
>
> Just about each invention had been anticipated, perhaps not 100 years in advance, but certainly at least a few years or even decades before, as in the case of the atomic bomb or the microchip.
>
> So, here planning is possible, even if one cannot forecast the precise day or year when the appropriate breakthrough occurs…. Predictability thus exists to the extent that the probability of certain inventions can be accelerated by resource deployment and favorable basic conditions. (Schrader, 1996, p. 6)

Another invention—the personal computer—shifts the focus of the question and raises another issue that figures prominently in our book: namely, the role of uncertainty in the innovation process.

Suddenly, the focus is no longer on the technical invention, but the *use* of the invention is at the center. Hence, it is about its exploitation, its utilization.... And so we are into the domain of innovation, where the largest unpredictability exists: the domain of an invention's utilization. Humans use their inventions differently than planned.... In the 1940s, one could probably foresee the enormous potential for efficiency with computers. No one counted on computers being used later for keeping recipes or as gaming equipment for children and adults....

The planning of innovations has two dimensions: the invention and its utilization. One thinks, intuitively, that it is with the invention that major uncertainty lies. But that is not correct at all. Big, basic uncertainties often exist with respect to utilization. Technical progress is still relatively foreseeable. The employment of an invention is substantially more difficult to predict.

Now let us look at how this works out in practice. What is actually planned in the context of innovation management? Here you may be surprised. Enterprises have relatively good capabilities when it comes to forecasting technological developments. There is a systematic monitoring of technology, watching of trends, and so on. This technicians manage. They appreciate inventions....

But we have neglected the innovation *process*. We ask, therefore, the final question: Can innovation *processes* be planned? For the operations manager, this is a major challenge. We can steer and arrange processes quite well that we *understand*. But an innovation is different. It is tied to the creation of something new. It is difficult to define tasks because we do not yet know which ones will be required....

We have learned that innovation covers two activities: the invention and its utilization. Both activities are not completely plannable, but this is more so with respect to utilization than with invention. We learn from this that despite the difficulty of planning, it is incorrect to conclude that the innovation process cannot be *managed*. (Schrader, 1996, pp. 6–7)

We show that both organizational structure and space are tools that can be used to manage the innovation process, as illustrated in Figure 1-1.

Every organization has a spatial dimension, and most space has an organizational dimension. People organize themselves to get things done and need space within which to do those things. We think in terms of space, and space takes on its real meaning by virtue of how it is used. Both organizational structure and space influence the interaction patterns among people, which are central to the innovation process. Bring the two together, and the manager has a better, more effective way of structuring interaction patterns that lead to innovation.

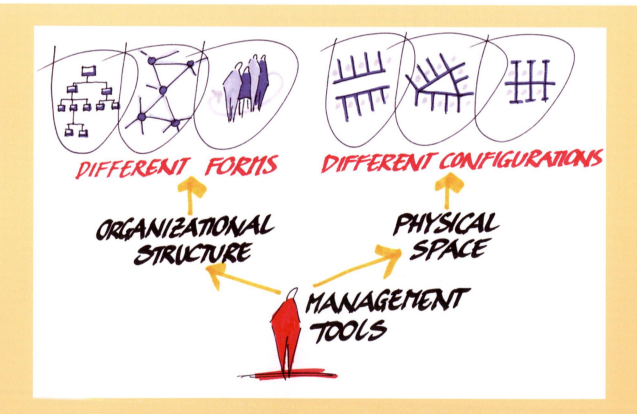

Figure 1-1 Managers should realize that they have both organizational structure and physical space available to them when planning the innovation process.

Much of our discussion focuses on *communication*[1]—for a very simple and direct reason. Earlier research by one of the present authors (Allen 1984) shows clearly the critical nature of internal technical communication in the new product innovation process. Innovation depends on invention and ideas, and this and other research finds consistently that the best source of new technical ideas for product development engineers is a colleague in the same organization (Figure 1-2).

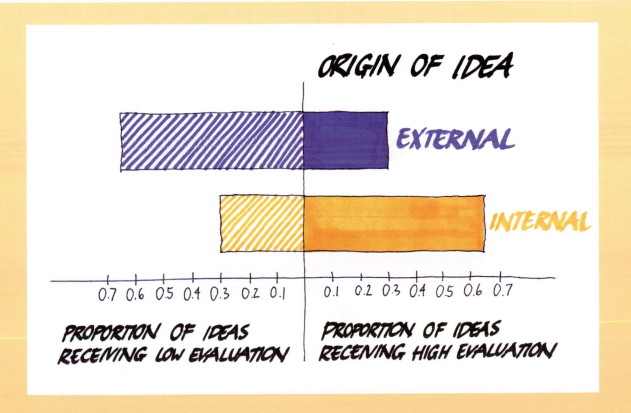

Figure 1-2 Most frequently, the best source of new technical ideas for product development engineers is a colleague in the same organization.

This rich source of ideas is significantly underutilized. Why? The research highlights many reasons, paramount among them being a simple lack of *awareness*. In large organizations, the staff is frequently unaware of the diversity of talent among their coworkers. We have heard so many stories from so many different people of how they searched far and wide for someone with a particular type of knowledge only to find that the right person was working within their own organizations, perhaps in an adjacent building. This is one important aspect of awareness, among several others, that we address.

As products grow in complexity, their development requires the efforts of larger numbers of people. These efforts extend well beyond the engineers or scientists who are assigned directly to product development; many others support the development through formal and informal consulting and contribute knowledge and ideas to the members of the development team. Given this need for additional technical support, it becomes essential to realize the maximum benefit from the communication processes within product development organizations.

The recognition of this need launched an extended program of research directed toward improving our understanding of what governs technical communication in organizations. We quickly uncovered three factors that determine the structure of technical communication networks in organizations. The first is the structure of the formal organization, which is reflected in organizational charts. We group people in organizational units (the boxes on a typical organizational chart) because we believe that communication among them will be productive. The second is the physical structure and layout of the facilities in which the work is performed, which brings us into the realm of architecture. The third is the structure of informal relations, sometimes referred to as an informal organizational structure, that develops among any set of people working in the same part of an organization or in proximity of one another.[2]

In all of these technical communication structures, awareness is important. In fact, awareness is a critical factor in the innovation process because of how the nature of work has changed and the impact that knowledge now has on work.

A century ago, the impact of knowledge on work was quite different. The typical organization had a division of labor; the work of its employees was divided into multiple parts. The results of each person's work were simply added together to create the resultant product. Only the bosses—foremen and executives—required the knowledge that allowed for a complete picture of the work. Individual workers did not need to know much more than what was specific to their individual tasks to complete their jobs.

Today, in the innovation-driven organization, the resource of knowledge is required in the work of nearly everyone. The results of each individual's work are not brought together at the end of a linear process, but are communicated throughout the process. Further, with respect to the product *development* process itself, growing numbers of people are involved in generating ideas and bringing those ideas together. Innovation is complex and unfolds in many steps, both big and small. Everyone must be up-to-date with respect to information, and all must coordinate their work—both of which impose on the organizational structure in a variety of ways. The dispersion of knowledge has been greatly aided by the ability to communicate information and knowledge via the Internet and by other rapid means. But these technological tools do not themselves resolve the challenges of managing the innovation process.

Innovation today results from collaboration and collective intelligence. The innovation process transcends individuals and transcends departments, with knowledge emerging within multiple disciplines. To succeed, it requires organizational structure for the sharing of knowledge and for inspired communication to unfold in real time, and the space that makes it possible. The organizational structure must be flexible to allow for the interactions that matter, and the space too must be supportive. They are co-equal partners in moving the innovation process forward and are essential to responding to its exigencies.

Organizations and their space need to respond to different requirements depending on where in the innovation process the work is unfolding. Organizations go through cycles of centralization and decentralization. They need a mix of organizational forms at any one time: individuals working on specific tasks, groups of individuals coming together for long-term projects or for quick discussions, and so on. The structure of a successful innovation organization is rarely stable, but is dynamic. It changes with the times and with what is needed.

Most managers will likely acknowledge the critical role played by organizational structure in the innovation process, but few understand that physical space is *equally* important. It has a tremendous influence on how and where communication takes place, on the quality of that communication, and on the movement—and hence, all interactions—of people within an organization. In fact, some of the most prevalent design elements of buildings nearly shut down the opportunities for the organizations that work within their walls to thrive and innovate. Hence, the implications of physical space for the innovation process are profound, as becomes clear when the different types of communication and their impact on innovation are understood (we discuss this in detail in Chapter 2).

There are numerous examples of physical space being designed to enhance communication and awareness. In some cases, the designs are complex and all encompassing. In others, they are simple and relatively straightforward reconfigurations of parts of buildings. One example of the latter can be found at the headquarters of a European manufacturing company, where the senior management committee understood that *creativity* must reign in any organization that is seeking to be innovative. However, the company's highly formal organizational structure grouped employees in silos and stifled certain types of communication. Even the senior management committee itself suffered from this problem, where boundaries exacerbated cross-functional communication.

The physical space for the company's senior management committee reflected the silos in the form of a single row of private offices, like that depicted in Figure 1-3, for each senior manager. Their movements and communication would proceed in a linear manner, from one person to the next. One executive had to "decide"—that is, make a conscious choice—to interact with another executive. His communication was structured hierarchically, which presents difficulties for coordination and information and essentially quashes inspiration.

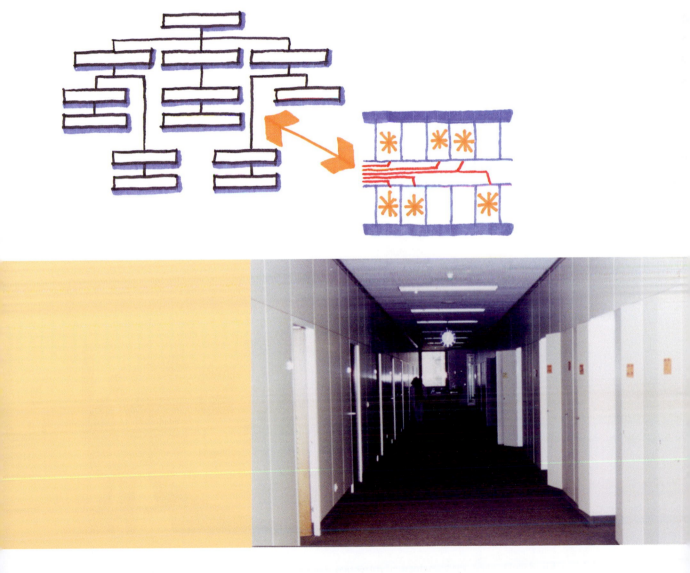

Figure 1-3 Physical space like that in the photograph reflects the silo organization depicted in the figure.

The process of resolving this dilemma began with physical space, which was configured to influence the ways in which people behave. A closed workspace was transformed (Figure 1-4) into an open space to encourage all types of communication. There was no change in the

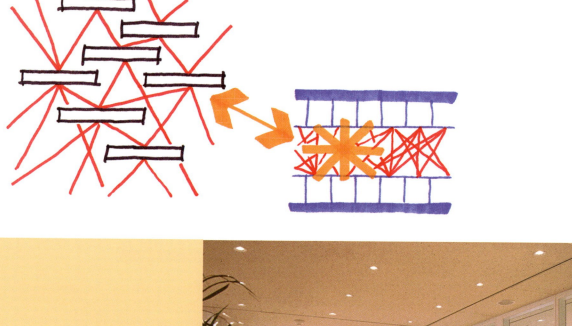

Figure 1-4 Closed workspace was transformed into open space to encourage all types of communication, as required by the organization depicted in the figure.

organizational chart or in specific reporting relationships; rather, the newly configured space influences the members of the senior management committee to reduce formality and silo-imposed isolation in their interactions. The new workspace allows senior managers—who represent all the functional areas of the corporation—to interact in ways that previously had been atypical, if not impossible.

The new configuration of space corresponds to the new way of thinking that the senior management committee wanted to promote as part of its own work. As Figure 1-4 illustrates, the first principle was to show management as a unified whole. While the executives can retreat to their private offices, the glass walls ensure that they remain visible to everyone in the vicinity. This is an important component of personal interaction, open communication, and awareness of *leadership*—that these executives lead the company and that their decisions can and should be made not in isolation, but as part of that unified whole.

The transparency indicated by windows both to the outside and inside is a metaphor for an orientation in different directions and is meant to support the idea that one has the freedom to make one's own decisions—that is, within the realm for which one is responsible—but also to influence the decisions of others seen through the glass walls. In terms of promoting interaction among senior management in a silo organization, this ability goes beyond being merely symbolic to being part and parcel of transforming the firm and its decision-making processes.

Another key element is the shared, or common, space. This space pulls the executives out from their offices and into the possibility of encounters with their colleagues and employees who are visiting from other parts of the building or from nearby manufacturing facilities. In the less-formal setting of a comfortable couch or a coffee bar, the company benefits from the chance conversations, sharing of ideas, and overall interaction that was far less likely to have taken place with the old, closed space configuration.

One important note about the European manufacturing company is that the transformation took place using the same physical space. No more or fewer square meters were used, but the configuration of the space changed completely.

To be sure, open space is not a panacea, but it does offer advantages—as the preceding example shows. Another example of its benefits is found at the MIT Sloan School of Management. The offices of faculty, graduate students, postdoctoral fellows, and visitors are grouped around a large open area (Figure 1-5). This area is designed for interaction and communication and has worked extremely well for many years. There is regular and effective communication among the faculty and with graduate students and through chance encounters with others who walk through the space on their way to another part of the building, or to take advantage of the free coffee and a comfort-

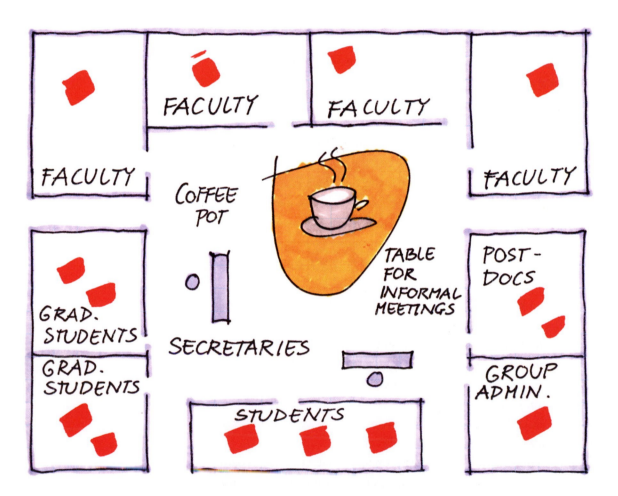

Figure 1-5 People have a reason to come to this open space, and the space allows for interaction and communication.

able sitting place. What at first glance may look like wasted space (and does to some of the people responsible for MIT's facilities management) is, in fact, more effective than the surrounding office space.

A major element of what the spaces at Sloan and the European manufacturer offer their users is *possibility*, which is part and parcel of the innovation process. A formal organizational structure may dictate what is *supposed* to happen, but whether it actually does happen is, in large part, an issue of space. Organizations need space where things can happen, where it is possible for the unexpected to unfold. It is in the less formal, open spaces such as these two locations—and in other buildings depicted in later chapters—where the chance encounters that are so important to the innovation process can take place. These are the spaces where hierarchical reporting lines are challenged, so that the possibility of developing innovative ideas can take place outside the restraint of some predetermined notion of how information might be shared.

These two spaces, again, are relatively simple approaches to using open space and room configuration to enhance communication and awareness. In later chapters, we discuss several other buildings in greater detail, and we detail the concept of "centers of gravity" that can be used to promote—or which may deter—interaction among groups or individuals. In these other examples, interaction is promoted by the ways in which space and flow are ordered so that the activities of individuals and groups unfold dynamically.

While it is questionable whether the builder had this in mind, an example of this approach can be found in the main buildings at MIT, in what has come to be known as the "Infinite Corridor." It is a central spine from which other corridors stem out perpendicularly to offices, classrooms, and laboratories. During the brief periods between class sessions, the traffic along this corridor can be quite heavy. Even at other times, people are drawn into this corridor to travel to other points within the buildings—but always with a deliberate destination. In fact, nearly every member of the staff, faculty, and student body on the main part of the MIT campus passes through the Infinite Corridor at least once each day. In this way, it is an important center of activity for MIT.

The concept of a *spine* as we use it here requires some explanation. A spine has both form and function. In the case of the MIT Infinite Corridor, the spinal *form* is obvious—a long hallway. Our concern is more with the *function* of the spine—as in the human body, where it is the conduit of the central nervous system. The spines in the buildings described below are the nerve centers of the physical space. Everyone is connected to the spines in some way, and it is to the spines that people in the buildings are attracted. It is along the spine that awareness of the most important activities takes place.[3]

The MIT Infinite Corridor is a very limited, and unintentional, example of how a spine functions. An even better example can be found in Gunter Henn's Faculty of Mechanical Engineering building at the Technical University of Munich, opened in May 1997. In this case, the building is structured like a city, and the space was consciously created for *meandering*, not only as a means to get from one place to another. Seven institutes of the Faculty of Mechanical Engineering are arranged on a 220-meter long enclosed "street" (Figure 1-6) that defines the building's spine, where students, faculty, and staff have the highest probability of meeting other people and exchanging ideas.

Figure 1-6 The "street" at the Technical University of Munich forms a spine through the middle of the complex of offices, laboratories, and classrooms and enables contacts among occupants.

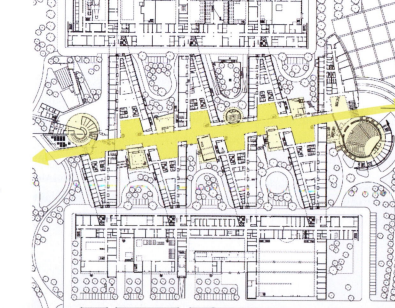

The importance of people's ability to meander through the spine cannot be understated; it is the means by which awareness of *learning* is promoted. The intention is clearly to promote networking interactions among groups and individuals who, like their counterparts at MIT, otherwise spend much of their time in offices. In this building, general openness allows visual contact to a very large and effective degree, even between floors, thus promoting a degree of awareness of people and activities seldom found in such a large building. Students and faculty can meet and network along the "street." The Technical University of Munich is discussed in much greater detail in Chapter 4.

Another example can be seen in Gunter Henn's Skoda automotive assembly plant in the Czech Republic (Figure 1-7), opened in 1996. Managers work in a block of offices along the central spine, surrounded by the production line. The center of activity is the interaction between managers and workers on the line, and the physical space enables this interaction at a very high level.

Figure 1-7 The Skoda assembly plant in Mladá Boleslav, Czech Republic, provides for visual contact and awareness between those in the center offices and those working on the assembly line.

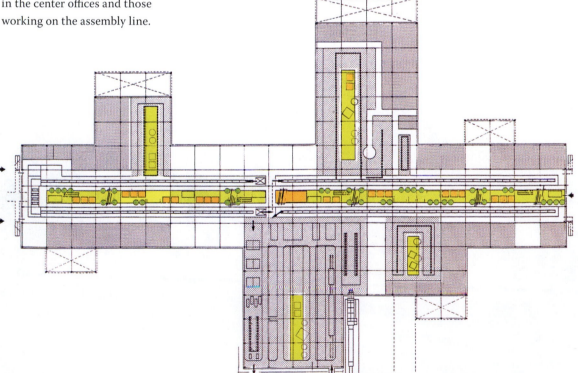

Detailed in Chapter 4, the factory is an example of using space to meet Skoda's objectives of increasing awareness of *quality* and *the nature of the actual production process.* The locus of awareness is situated along the production line. People who once were physically separated—and whose knowledge is intimately linked in the design and production processes related to the product—are now together in the same physical space and in constant visual contact with the production process. Their awareness of that process happens in *real time.*

Yet another variety of the spine concept can be found in Gunter Henn's BMW Projekthaus (Figure 1-8), opened in Munich in 2004, discussed in detail in Chapter 5. In this instance, the spine is vertical, and the placement in the center of prototype cars—in other words, BMW's innovation projects—creates a center of gravity that is multidimensional. The location of project work proximal to this central nervous system draws people and activities. Staff members located within the departmental offices peripheral to the Projekthaus are drawn across the bridges to participate in the work of the project (coordination and information). Here, they encounter other staff from different projects and product lines, thus increasing the potential for inspirational communication. The Projekthaus promotes awareness of BMW's *innovation process.*

The Projekthaus shows that physical space can be configured specifically to complement the organizational structure of those who work within it. At the same time, the building allows for a dynamic approach to organizational structure; the physical space can be changed according to what projects need. In this way, the Projekthaus organizational structure and physical space together comprise an optimized system.

Figure 1-8 The BMW Projekthaus in Munich, Germany, provides flexible space for a matrixed product development organization.

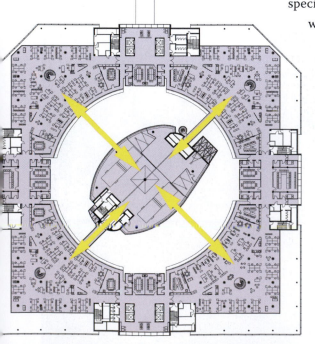

All of these aspects of spatial configuration figure into our discussion in later chapters. To understand better the link between organizational structure and space, we must first understand the flow of communication and the evolution of organizational structures that have led us to identify organization and space as such critical tools for the innovation process. Chapter 2 begins our detailed exploration of these topics.

Notes

[1] In this book, we concentrate on *face-to-face* communication, a limitation that may seem absurd in the twenty-first century. As we move on, however, it will become obvious that communication through modern media seldom substitutes for face-to-face communication. Rather, the use of different media (including face-to-face) is more likely to be positively correlated, and they augment, not substitute, for one another. We do, nevertheless, discuss telecommunications briefly in Chapter 3.

[2] The words "working in the same part of an organization or in proximity" demonstrate the effect formal organization and physical layout have on informal relations. True, they are not the only determinants, but their effect—while not absolute—is strong enough to stimulate us to consider the effects of organizational and physical space on technical communication.

[3] Gunter Henn, one of the authors of this book and the architect of the three buildings that are described in the remainder of this chapter and in Chapters 4 and 5, is the innovator of the application of this specific spine concept.

References

Allen TJ (1984). *Managing the flow of technology: Technology transfer and the dissemination of technological information within the R&D organization.* Cambridge, MA: MIT Press.

Schrader S (1996). Die Planbarkeit von Innovationen. *Henn Akademie Proceedings* 1, January 24, 1996.

Schumpeter JA (1934). *The theory of economic development.* Cambridge, MA: Harvard University Press. (First published in German in 1911.)

2

The Process of Innovation

A S WE LEARNED IN CHAPTER 1, innovation itself cannot be predicted, but the innovation process can be managed. It requires interaction among people, and as a creative process it presupposes that people will come upon the unexpected. An organization's knowledge also matters in the process,[1] and the tasks associated with managing knowledge have major implications for organizational structure.

A critical success factor in the innovation process requires at least that the organization be able to access, maintain, and *transfer* knowledge from person to person. To understand how this knowledge transfer works, we must understand the different types of communication among engineers and scientists in organizations.

Types of Communication

Restricting our consideration only to the technical and scientific communication upon which innovation so depends, we find three types (Allen 1986). Each serves a different purpose.

The first type is *communication for coordination*. This type of communication exists in nearly all organizations; there has to be communication to coordinate work. As the adage goes: "The right hand has to know what the left hand is doing." In an engineering environment, for instance, we might say that the parts or subsystems must work together compatibly. The engineers designing those components or subsystems must, therefore, remain familiar with each other's progress in design. This is the purpose of communication for coordination.

The second type is *communication for information*. This type of communication ensures that we "keep up-to-date" with new developments in our scientific and technical areas of expertise. Communication for information increases in importance with the rate at which knowledge is changing in any given discipline or technology.

The third type is *communication for inspiration*. Unlike communication for information, which serves the role of transferring and transforming existing knowledge, communication for inspiration is active in *creating knowledge*. In an organization that relies on creative solutions to problems, communication for inspiration is absolutely critical. It is usually spontaneous and often occurs between people who work in different organizational units, on different projects, while drawing from different disciplines. These communicators are people who, under normal circumstances, would have little to do with each other and perhaps not interact at all. It is cross-disciplinary, cross-functional communication that allows the development of unusual combinations of ideas that lead to imagination and creativity. Because of these characteristics, it is also the most unpredictable and, hence, the most difficult type of communication to manage.

"Harnessing" communication for inspiration has implications for successfully creating knowledge. But it also implies crossing the boundaries of organizational structure. While managers generally recognize the need for interunit communication within the organization, they are often at a loss to promote it. Consequently, there is frequently very poor communication among subunits. In addition, we too often assume that all communication needs are reflected in the way the organization is structured. The conventional wisdom is that *organizational structure* creates the complete means by which knowledge can be shared and exploited for a firm's benefit. However, organizational structure has its limitations.

When we look at a variety of organizations, we find that the need for communication for coordination and information is usually well represented by the organizational structure. Senior managers devote an inordinate amount of time and attention to structuring organizational units and carefully crafting relationships among those units. We see this most prominently in product development.2 There, decisions on whether to locate engineers and scientists in departments or project teams and how to relate these units to one another in structures such as the organizational matrix can be critical to managing cost, schedule, and product performance. What becomes of paramount concern is organizational "location." What we rarely find, though, is an organizational structure designed specifically to manage communication for inspiration. Here, physical space can come to the rescue. The configuration of space can allow for the "uncertainty" in interactions that lead to inspiration—something organizational structure can seldom accomplish.

A notable example of using both space and organizational structure to promote communication for inspiration can be found in the laboratory of Hallmark in Kansas City, Missouri. The greeting card company employs artists to create the basic ideas for its products. It also requires engineers to design the processes by which their artistic products can be mass produced. Despite being organized separately, these two very different kinds of people must communicate effectively. Hallmark resolved this dilemma in part by establishing common space in its facility to be shared by these two groups, which typically would have a very low level of interaction. The features in this common space go well beyond a coffee machine and a copier. Because the common space is set up as a kind of "playground," Hallmark artists and engineers are attracted to a center of activity where they truly enjoy spending time thinking and conversing.

Organizations that depend for their success on creating knowledge but concentrate on the first two types of communication and ignore the centrality of communication for inspiration do so at their own risk. In the knowledge-driven organization there is always a need for all three types of communication we've identified.

Put more bluntly, it is not enough to coordinate and share information. Communication for inspiration stimulates creativity, one of the fundamental bases of innovation. Often, it is the initial source of new ideas for solving problems and for products and services. In other words, it is an absolutely essential part of the innovation *process*. It stands to reason, then, that if communication for inspiration can be encouraged and harnessed, it ought to have a positive impact on an organization's innovativeness.

Let's look at how organizations have structured themselves to do their work, ensure that knowledge *is* transferred, and—they hope—innovate. From there, we will be able to address more specifically the role of physical space in the innovation process.

The Evolution of Organizational Structure

A simple depiction of innovation is one of a process that mediates between two streams of activity: the development of market needs and the development of technological capabilities or potential solutions to meet those market needs (Figure 2-1).

Typically, organizations that structure themselves to function with one stream of activity find the challenges far less daunting than when they try to organize to address both streams of activity simultaneously. This is true because of the different nature of the two streams and because of what past practice has wrought. Historically, product development organizations aligned themselves first with the technology stream, grouping technological knowledge into disciplines or specialties that came to be labeled "technologies." These disciplines were structured hierarchically into subspecialties, sub-subspecialties, and so on. Figure 2-2 expands Figure 2-1, showing this structure of an organization by department (D1, D2, etc.) around technology specialties/subspecialties, with a solid tie to the technology stream of activity.

Figure 2-1 The innovation process mediates between the development of market needs and the development of technological capabilities. It assesses market needs, applies technological capabilities to meet those needs, and provides new products to the market while advancing technology.

Technology

Innovation

Market

Figure 2-2 The innovation process can be organized by departments built around technological specialties, similar to the common organizational structure in academic institutions.

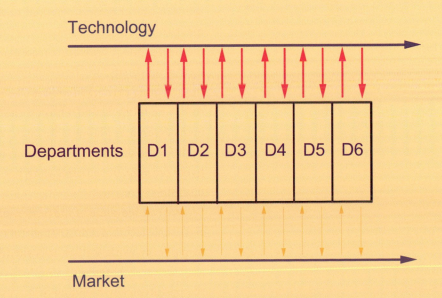

Technology

Departments | D1 | D2 | D3 | D4 | D5 | D6

Market

Earlier, we mentioned that making sure technical staff can keep in close contact with new developments within their specialties is very important to knowledge management. Research shows that for engineers the dissemination of technical knowledge happens mostly through face-to-face contact. Departmental organization, because it groups together people who share the same area of specialized knowledge, enables them to communicate more readily with each other and keep one another informed of new developments. Thus, departmental organization provides an effective coupling to those areas of technology represented in its structure (Allen 1986).

The origins of this form of organization are in the university. Since the twelfth century, universities have been largely organized around specialized areas of knowledge. This was virtually cast in stone by Wilhelm and Alexander von Humboldt in their establishment and later development of the University of Berlin in the early nineteenth century. The departments of chemistry, physics, mechanical engineering, history, mathematics, and so on in today's modern university are reflected in the software, signal processing, mechanical structures, materials, and other departments in the modern product development organization. Within each discipline in the university, we find subgroupings representing subspecialties, creating clusters of individuals who share common intellectual roots and interests and who can share knowledge gained from their own research or obtained through contact with external colleagues in the same discipline. The system has worked because, until relatively recently, universities were not called upon to do much cross-disciplinary research.

We can see some of the limitations of this model for industry in the simple fact that industry has not had the luxury of avoiding cross-disciplinary work. Rather, it is the norm in industry. Today's products are rarely based on a single discipline, as was more common in the past; typically, blending or integrating knowledge from different and sometimes disparate specialties is necessary today to develop even relatively simple products.

When industry created R&D laboratories, they emulated the university system that the engineers and scientists knew best, following the pattern of creating specialized departments organized around specialized areas of knowledge. But soon this organizational structure proved to be an obstacle to relating effectively to the market (which is why the connections to the market in Figure 2-2 are thinner). To use an idiom from engineering, there is an "impedance mismatch" on the market side of the model with respect to the transfer of information.

The reason for this mismatch is relatively simple: The market and technology are organized differently. Market needs are defined in the form of products and services and do not necessarily align with technological specialties or disciplines. In fact, they usually draw knowledge from a variety of disciplines or technologies, thus requiring an integration of knowledge from varied sources.

Remember, the departmental structure does assure that technical staff can keep in close contact with new developments within their specialties. But it's weak on combining or integrating knowledge from different specialties to develop a new product. That requires *coordination* among the specialists, each of whose work or approach can have a serious effect on the work of other specialists. They must keep one another informed of what they are doing, often on a regular and quite frequent basis.

Organization by specialty—the departmental structure—is not well suited to meeting this challenge. Coordinating work across departmental divisions can be very difficult, exacerbated by the fact that specialists are reporting to different bosses and are often physically separated. The failure to communicate—which results from this structure but is not deliberate—results from the specialists not seeing each other regularly, and therefore not understanding what each cog in the wheel is doing.

One approach to this problem is nonorganizational: Extend the time dedicated to the development of the product. Time can always be substituted for coordination; given infinite time, no coordination is needed (a point illustrated by Figure 2-3). Stages in the development can always be repeated until, finally, compatibility among all aspects is achieved. Historically, this approach was used in some industries such as pharmaceuticals, for example, where coordination is particularly difficult. The converse is also true. Reducing development time increases the premium on coordination. That is why as the pharmaceutical industry has come under greater pressure of this sort, it has tended to adopt the *organizational* solution found by other industries faced with this coordination problem—namely, to create project teams.

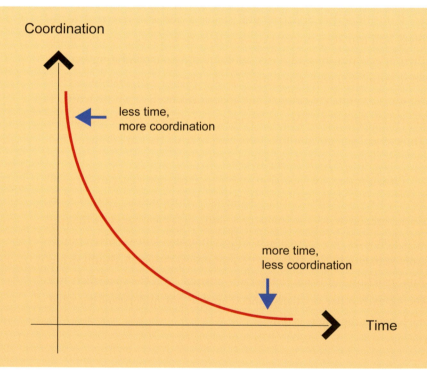

Figure 2-3 Time can always be substituted for coordination in the innovation process and, given infinite time, no coordination is necessary.

With the project team solution, specialists are removed (at least temporarily) from their departments and grouped together under a common boss (Figure 2-4). They then live together in this new organizational structure while their talents are needed to develop the new product or service. Since they are more likely to see each other regularly, coordination is made easier.

The price of this different approach is illustrated in Figure 2-4: a less-solid tie to the technology stream of activity. The specialists have been separated from their knowledge bases. While they can now communicate more readily with others engaged in the same development, accomplishing that has made it more difficult to stay in close communication with colleagues within their own specialty.[3]

The result is that the specialists are less likely to stay informed and up-to-date with respect to new developments within their specialties. They focus almost exclusively on the peculiar aspects of their technology in the context of a particular project and soon lose sight of other applications and developments in that technology. They are more likely to fall behind in the "state-of-the-art" in their respective specialized areas of knowledge. Remember, colleague contact has been shown repeatedly to be the most effective way of keeping technical professionals abreast of current knowledge (Allen 1984).

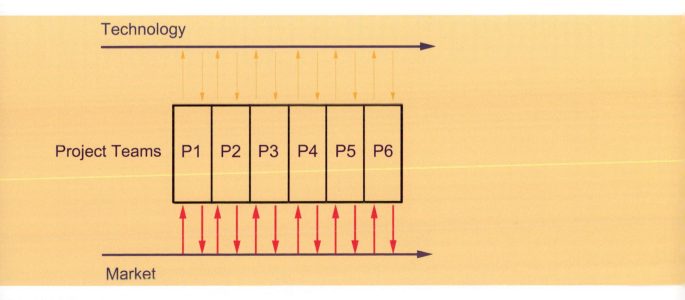

Figure 2-4 Another way to organize the innovation process is to remove specialists from their departments and group them together in project teams.

When Teams Remain Together Too Long

An additional problem can arise if the project team remains together for too long. While there is normally a period during which the team improves its performance through "team building," performance eventually plateaus and, quite often, it subsequently decays (Figure 2-5) (Pelz and Andrews 1966; Katz and Allen 1982).

The separation of individuals from their disciplinary knowledge bases creates a problem in reassigning the resulting prematurely "obsolete" staff to new projects. They are "behind the times" technically and won't be bringing the best of current knowledge to the new assignment. Second, and more serious, this effect can be spread across a wide portion of the staff if the organization adopts project team organization too widely. When a large proportion of the technical staff of an organization falls behind in knowledge, the organization itself falls behind. Thus, we find that too widespread use of project team structure can lead to an erosion of a company's knowledge base.

Research attributes the performance decay to what has come to be known as the "Not Invented Here" attitude that teams often develop. Team members come to believe that they have a monopoly on the world's knowledge in their product area and cease seeking new knowledge from outside their membership. This can be disastrous, as Figure 2-5 shows.

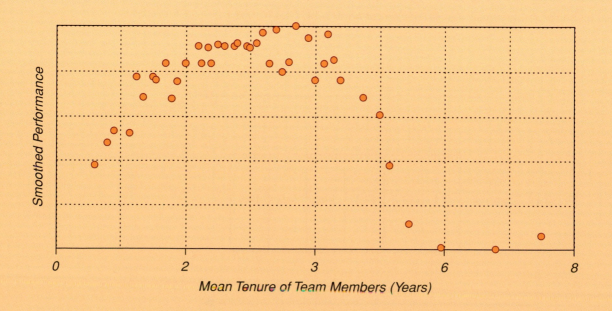

Figure 2-5 Project Performance as a Function of Team Age (45 Chemical Industry Projects)

What was the next stage in the evolution of organizational structure? The *matrix* organization evolved because project teams, while making intense focus and coordination possible, could not meet the challenge of keeping technical staff in close contact with new developments within their specialties. It traces its origins back to the late 1950s, when T. Wilson of the Boeing Company tried to accomplish both with a new organizational form for a major aerospace development program. The organization he devised later came to be known as "the matrix." It is an organizational structure that typically uses functional supervisors and project supervisors to manage the same people, depending on the assignment, and share the responsibility of assigning priorities. Lines of responsibility go in at least two directions in the matrix organization. In the matrix form of organization, project teams and departments are supposed to interact in a way that accomplishes the necessary coordination, while maintaining current knowledge in the relevant technologies and their connections to the market (Figure 2-6).

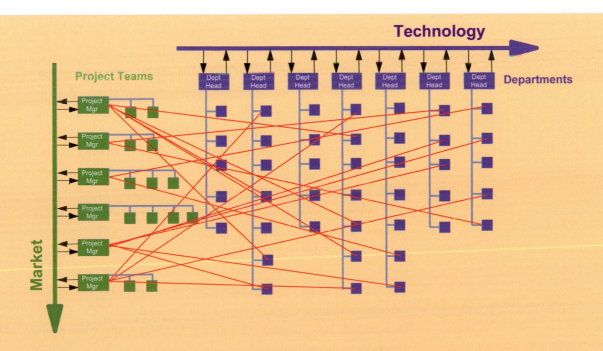

Figure 2-6 In this matrix organization, the blue area comprises departments with subgroups, and the green boxes are project teams. The red lines represent matrix relations.

The idea behind the matrix organization is correct, at least in theory, but anyone who has worked in such an organization will testify that it doesn't always function quite so neatly. Almost as soon as the matrix form of organizational structure was "invented," objections were raised. Many asked how people could work for multiple bosses—the project leader and the department head. However, this is only one of the problems.

Among project managers in the matrix organization, there usually develops a high level of competition for resources—because all such managers tend to think that their project is the organization's most crucial. Among the resources for which they compete, none is seen as more important than *talent*, embodied in people. Managers want the best people on their projects. The fierce competition that erupts over talent can be destructive for an organization if left unmanaged, so someone must establish priorities—which is an ongoing process, since priorities are dynamic and require constant monitoring. If priorities are not managed in a matrix organization, the organization will self-destruct.

From the point of view of department heads, there's a different problem. As the matrix matures, power tends to shift to the project side, since the project teams are responsible for getting out products. Senior management tends to focus on this aspect of the work, since creativity at the conceptual level—while valued—does not have so readily obvious a return. Department managers sense this shift, and they tend to resist anything that solidifies the matrix organization—even to the point of resisting its creation in the first place. From their perspective, the matrix leaves them with little to do other than manage a labor pool.

This situation of how senior management tends to view the project side of the equation is exacerbated by the pressure project managers come under from the marketing function of the organization and perhaps even from key customers. Even if a product isn't "ready," the pressure to get it to market can be tremendous because of what the competition is doing or is perceived to be doing. If the competitors already have released their next generation product, the project manager's job can be in jeopardy. The fear of losing market share drives much of the pressure—which can result in a product being released to the market prematurely.

Organizations can prevent this situation by restoring the authority of the departmental side of the matrix and making department heads responsible for product integrity, functioning as a countering force, a conservative force to ensure that a product is ready. Of course, if they become too powerful in this function, the problem swings back to the other side, and the product is held back for too long. Engineers have a fundamental drive always to improve the product and incorporate new features or improve on old ones.[4] Department heads are often driven in the same manner. So, we don't want to go too far in either direction; balance is critical.

The Revenge of the Department Heads

One of the authors was visited a few years ago by the director of the agricultural research institute in one of the Organisation for Economic Co-operation and Development (OECD) countries. His institute was organized, as are most such institutes, in a departmental structure reflecting the several long-established areas of agricultural research. In the director's view, this old form of organization was inadequate to deal with the modern problems of energy and environmental conservation. He believed he needed a form of matrix organization, and he was probably right. However, he was also wise enough to realize that his department heads would bitterly oppose such a change. He claimed to have a solution. He would implement an extreme strategy: eliminate all of the departments and then establish long-term project teams, to which he would assign all the scientists. Some of the "former" department heads could make good project managers, and they would be so assigned. Those who could not would be dealt with in some other way. Then, after leaving this form of organizational structure in place for some sufficient length of time, the director planned to re-establish the departments. This would, in essence, bring the matrix in "through the back door." The author wished him luck and awaited word of the outcome.

The answer came two years later when a letter arrived from the gentleman. Oddly, he made no mention of the agricultural institute or what happened with the organizational structure. The answer, however, was evident in the letterhead. He was now teaching in a university, and the likelihood is that the department heads were still running their departments back in the agricultural institute just as they had always done. The only change was that the director was now gone.

This need for balance can create a high degree of ongoing contention between project teams and departments, and particularly between project managers and department heads. Figure 2-7 illustrates what we refer to as a "battle zone," where the tensions come precisely from these pressures and from serving two "bosses"—in the project team and in the department. In long-term projects, these problems are made even worse because people find themselves increasingly separated from their departments and the knowledge base of their disciplines, while still being tied to them within the organizational structure.

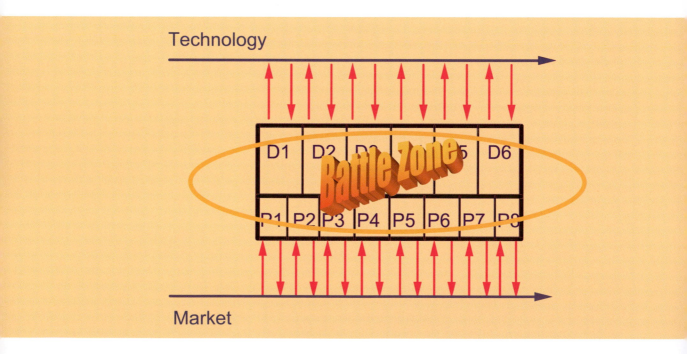

Figure 2-7 The matrix organizational structure is not without challenges. Tensions arise from pressures felt at the departmental level and within the project teams, as well as from the feeling people have that they must serve two "bosses."

The conflict in the "battle zone" is an absolutely necessary part of making the matrix work to advantage and realizing the best outcome from this organizational structure. The optimal situation is the result of two forces within the matrix. One force should be working to get the product out into the market; the other force is holding back to guarantee product integrity. Product integrity is a major responsibility of departmental management. Conflict is, therefore, an inherent characteristic of a matrix organization. It is integral and intended to be there. It should not be eliminated, but managed. It is a sign that the matrix is truly working. Were there no conflict, it would be an indication that one side—be it departments or project teams—was dominant, and that would negate the matrix's potential effectiveness in the innovation process.

One key question with the use of the matrix organizational structure is which specialists should join the project team and which should be kept within the departments. Answering this question requires looking more deeply at the basic trade-off implied by these two forms of organization (Table 2-1).

Table 2-1 simply repeats what we have already noted: Departmental organization connects staff more effectively to their knowledge base at the cost of greater difficulty in coordinating their work with other specialists, whereas project team organization improves coordination at the cost of great difficulty in keeping abreast of new developments in the specialties.

A Common Mistake

Frequently, what are in reality long-term project teams come to be treated as departments and are so structured in organizational charts. This is a serious error because now the true departments that are the sources of technical support for projects no longer feel any obligation to support them. We have seen this phenomenon often.

Inquiring about a department that appears on a company's organizational chart, we will ask about its responsibilities. The answer will come back that they are responsible for this or that line of products. Such an organizational unit is not a department in the matrix organization sense, and should not be treated as a department. Such treatment will separate the unit and its activities from the company's bases of technical knowledge. It will also induce the unit to create its own knowledge sources by duplicating work that is, or should be, going on in the true departments.

TABLE 2-1 **The Organization Structure Trade-off**

Organization Type	Benefit	Cost
Departmental	Provides good technological support	Difficulty in coordinating work
Project Team	Promotes coordination of individual efforts	Decouples the effort from supporting technologies

When we look a little more deeply at this situation, we quickly realize that the degree of need for current knowledge is largely determined by the rate at which technology is changing. If a technology is not developing very rapidly, staying current is not very difficult. Those who work with mature, stable technologies are not as compelled to communicate with disciplinary colleagues to stay current. But the situation is very different with technologies that are changing rapidly. If new knowledge is being generated at a rapid rate, old knowledge becomes quickly outdated. Those who are working with fast-changing, dynamic technologies must sustain very strong colleague contact to maintain up-to-date knowledge, lest both the project and the organization suffer.

The degree to which coordination is needed varies, too. In some instances, specialists *must* maintain regular, frequent contact, even perhaps do their work in one another's presence or jointly. In other cases, specialists can work quite independently and inform others of what they've done periodically, perhaps even after extended time has passed. What determines the need for coordination is the degree of *interdependence* in a project. The interdependence can occur within the physical architecture of the product (interaction among subsystems or components) or in the nature of the development work (tasks that are dependent upon the completion of other tasks or that must be done simultaneously).

A project might have many subsystems, specialties, or problem areas and still not require much coordination. If the subsystems or problem areas are relatively independent (what engineers like to describe as "black boxes"5)—that is, a modular design—the specialists need not coordinate their work to the same degree as if the subsystems were highly interdependent. When a business decides on an organizational structure, therefore, it must take the degree of interdependence into account.

In determining the appropriate organizational structure, the two parameters we've already introduced—the rate of change of knowledge and interdependence—are but two among four. Another is *project duration* or, more precisely, the length of time that any specialist is assigned to work on the project. The longer an engineer or scientist is assigned to a project team, the longer that individual is disconnected from the specialist department. This means that a given specialist could fall behind on the current knowledge about a moderately dynamic technology when assigned to an exceptionally long project. Even very short project team assignments could cause specialists dealing with a highly dynamic technology to fall behind in their knowledge.

Standard Industrial Practice and the Three Dimensions of Organizational Structure

Standard industrial practice normally ignores the first two principles described in this chapter. First, the rate at which technologies are developing is almost never taken into account when considering the structure of a product development organization—despite the availability of a metric for this dimension. If one were to compare two technologies on the basis of rate of change, one could compare the journals devoted to each technology and determine the half-life of the citations in each. Citation half-life can be a useful surrogate for rate-of-change, and it is readily available through the Science Citation Index, which publishes this statistic annually for a wide range of scientific and engineering journals. The same comparison can be done for patent citations across patent categories. To our knowledge, the citation half-life statistic is not publicly available—which is unfortunate—and would have to be calculated.

Second, the *interdependencies* in product architecture or in the nature of the required tasks are, surprisingly, also seldom taken into account—with two exceptions. Experienced project managers learn that their principal responsibility is the *management of interdependencies*. They also learn, therefore, that there is often more than one way to partition a project into tasks. This may allow them to reduce the degree of interdependence, thus making their lives easier. The second exception involves the use of a very valuable tool called the Design Structure Matrix, or DSM (Eppinger et al. 1994; www.dsmweb.org). The DSM can be used to determine which tasks within each phase of a complex project should or should not be performed concurrently. It is an extremely useful tool for highlighting interdependencies in large, complex developments and has been shown to be very effective in managing costs and schedules. It is a clear recognition of the importance of assessing interdependencies when managing complex product developments.

The third dimension, *project duration*, is the one most often chosen in deciding upon an organizational structure. The problem, though, is that normal practice is to use this in exactly the wrong way. If a project's duration will be short, a departmental structure is chosen, because moving staff to a project team is seen as too disruptive over this relatively short period. For a longer development, a project team is usually formed. This is completely in opposition to the logic developed in this chapter.

An Objection

Some managers will raise an objection. They will claim that the staff on the majority of their development projects face both extremely high rates of technology change and high interdependence—and so neither departmental structure nor project team assignment will solve their problem. The solution to this dilemma is to time-sequence the movement of these staff between departmental and project team segments of the organization. At project initiation, it is best to integrate them into project teams. During this initial period, team building will occur. The team members come to know and understand each, and each other's specialties, better. They develop working relationships. They should not be left in teams too long, however, lest the problems discussed earlier in this chapter develop. They should then be dispersed to their home departments. The team-building phase will have its payoff at this time, and coordination across departments will be far easier. If the development is of very long duration, the process may be repeated.

Everything up to this point has been about the technology stream of activity, and the astute reader should rightly ask, "What about the market?" After all, it is an equal partner with technology in the model of the innovation process. In fact, it is the fourth parameter.

Just as technology changes, so do customers' and society's needs—in many different ways and at different rates. Markets, too, vary in their dynamism. Some market niches may be stable, with little change in requirements from year to year. Other markets are fluctuating rapidly and constantly. The implications for organizational structure are significant.

A shift or advance in technology can very often stimulate existing markets or open completely new ones. Jim Utterback (1974), in his meta-analysis of innovation studies, showed many years ago that the market provides the stimulus for about 70 percent of "commercially successful" innovations.6 Market dynamics can also affect project duration. Changes in the market can precipitate efforts to accelerate projects, through the commitment of increased resources.

The Trumpet Model of the Product Development Process and Physical Space

As the development of a product progresses, the process moves through a number of stages,7 as depicted in Figure 2-8—our Trumpet model of the product development process. Different organizations give these stages different names over time; our nomenclature is arbitrary.

During each stage, the nature of the work can be quite different. For example, in Phase I—the earliest stage—the work is generally more freewheeling and at the highest conceptual and creative level, often tied to an initial assessment of a market need. Phase I is usually relatively low cost, involving the fewest number of people. Physical space needs are minimal, as is the need for organizational controls (because there is not so much money at risk). In Phase I, a high degree of communication for inspiration is desired.

The development process reaches Phase II when the general structure of a product has been determined and the developers determine that what they're seeking to accomplish can, in fact, be done. At this point, the objective is to refine the design and scale up the concept to something that can be turned into a product that can be manufactured. When these goals have been met, the process shifts to Phase III. The design is frozen, and in Phase III one of the principal objectives is to work out the details of how the product will be manufactured.

In Phase I, practicality—a "restraint" often removed to promote creativity and innovative thought—does not yet assume the prominence it will later attain. However, when a preliminary design is achieved, practicalities must be brought to bear. While a prototype may not in a test have broken any of the laws of physics, the product is hardly ready for the market. It needs to be tested further to determine whether it will function in the environment that goes along with the market. Maintainability, flexibility, adaptability, robustness, and other "ilities" enter into the equation in Phase II; designing to meet these criteria may be necessary, which requires more people and more money and, hence, may require financial controls and tighter management (although applied too early, such controls could stifle innovativeness, so a delicate balance must be struck).

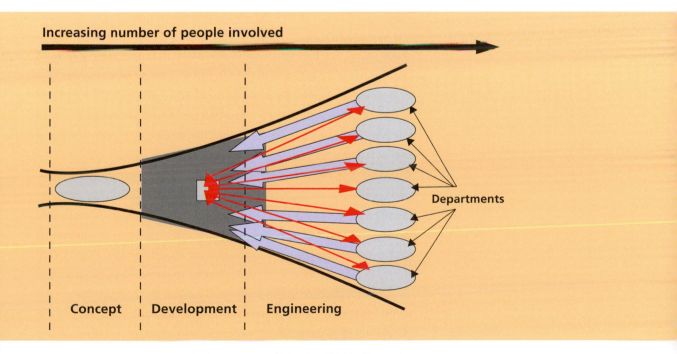

Figure 2-8 Trumpet Model of the Product Development Process

The different stages of the Trumpet model also represent inevitable organizational changes. At certain points, people will be working in a matrix arrangement under two very different "bosses"—namely, their departments and their teams. With larger numbers of engineers drawn from a variety of disciplines, the organizational structure must be able to promote coordination among them while still allowing them contact with their disciplinary colleagues. When the nature of the work, the numbers of people involved, and their "reporting" relationships reach this point, the *physical space* must augment and reinforce the matrix and enable the necessary coordination and information flow. From the architectural point of view, the facility must be flexible enough to accommodate the expansion we see in the figure, as well as the eventual contraction, and the change in the nature of the interaction.

In the earlier phase, when the team is small and the duration of its work may not last long, a smaller, perhaps flexible space works well. A small number of people may work creatively even to structure their space to be inspiring and reflect their particular social fabric. In other words, a small number of people are more likely to organize themselves and use space to their advantage.

The growing team in the commercial development stage needs more space, but that space must suit more than just the purpose of housing a larger number of people. In Phase II, space becomes a tool for organizing the "team" of people involved and—as the engineers in one of the teams with which we worked expressed it—"the project becomes the boss." It must be space that promotes intrateam coordination and makes it easier for engineers to contact their disciplinary colleagues—because it is in Phase II that the "battle zone" nature of the matrix organization, which we discussed above, plays out. Physical space in Phase II can be the tool for building awareness on every level. It allows people to interact in *real time*, without barriers. All three types of communication—including the communication for inspiration that is so vital to the innovation process—can take place at any time. Physical space can also make it possible to place the prototype of the new product at the center so that all of those involved in the innovation process see the development of the product and can react—again, in real time. In this way, knowledge—implicit, explicit, and intuitive—is made visual.

As the development progresses further into "engineering," the need for coordination increases, and the need for disciplinary support is somewhat less. The product design is relatively fixed or "frozen" by this point, and there is less need for team members to keep abreast of disciplinary knowledge. Interfunctional project teams gain greater prominence, and the development is managed through what are known as Integrated Product Teams (IPTs). The requirement for a large physical space remains, since the team usually continues to expand, but organizational structure rather than space once again becomes the key tool for managing the innovation process.

We have thus far followed only a single development, however. Larger companies usually have a number of developments underway simultaneously, each in a different stage of the process. That makes the space requirements much more difficult to meet. It also means that the physical space must be flexible enough to meet the needs of several expanding and contracting teams simultaneously. This is the basic thinking that underlies the design of BMW's Projekthaus (introduced in Chapter 1 and detailed in Chapter 5), where physical space designed specifically for Phase II of this Trumpet model functions as a tool with which the company can manage its innovation process.

In the next chapter, we explore precisely how communication flows in physical space and the impact this has on the innovation process. We also look at some cases in which companies addressed the challenges of creating an environment for innovation by specifically employing two management tools: organizational structure and physical space.

Notes

[1]   We see wide discussion of the issues surrounding intellectual property (IP). While IP is certainly a critical portion of an organization's knowledge, it is not the only part. A lot of knowledge may be widely shared but still be very important to any one organization. It is this broader sense of an organization's knowledge with which we are concerned.

[2]   In fact, many of the organizational forms now widely used across functions in industry, from project management to matrix organization, had their origin in product development organizations.

[3]   We are referring now to developments of what we might call "normal" size, in which there is a very limited number of individuals from any single specialty in the team. It does not apply as strongly to the very large projects, with hundreds of specialists engaged. These can often have a specialized functional organizational structure within the project team that allows for a "critical mass" of specialists within many of the specialties.

[4]   Just look at what has happened recently with mobile telephones.

[5]   A wonderful example can be found in the original IBM personal computer, the add-on boards of which were certainly "black boxes." As long as the design adhered to a minimal set of electrical and mechanical specifications, almost any feature could be designed into the board—with little or no interaction with the computer's "motherboard." This black box design stimulated many innovative ideas that were first incorporated in the add-on boards and later integrated into either the motherboard or the operating system software.

[6]   We must add that technology push is responsible for many of the more significant innovations of the recent past. Included in this set are several very important products that have completely changed markets or created entirely new markets. Consider the impact of the pocket calculator, the personal computer, or the personal digital assistant.

[7]   The actual number is debatable. Different authors have suggested numbers varying from two up. The fact is that the number and nature of stages will vary considerably depending on the industry and the nature of the individual project. In addition, the actual number may simply be in the eye of the beholder. At any rate, most will agree that there are multiple stages and that each has its own managerial and communication requirements.

References

Allen TJ (1984). *Managing the flow of technology: Technology transfer and the dissemination of technological information within the R&D organization*. Cambridge, MA: MIT Press.

Allen TJ (1986). Organizational structure, information technology and R&D productivity. *IEEE Transactions on Engineering Management* 33(4): 212–217.

Eppinger SD, Whitney DE, Smith RP, and Gebala DA (1994). A model-based method for organizing tasks in product development. *Research in Engineering Design* 6:1–13.

Katz R, and Allen TJ (1982). Investigating the Not Invented Here (NIH) syndrome: A look at the performance, tenure and communication patterns of 50 R&D project groups. *R&D Management* 12(1):7–19.

Pelz D, and Andrews F, eds. (1966). *Scientists in organizations: Productive climates for research and development.* New York: Wiley.

Utterback JM (1974). Innovation in industry and the diffusion of technology. *Science* 183:620–626.

3 The Flow of Communication in Space

THE PHYSICAL SPACE WITHIN WHICH people work strongly affects what occurs, and can occur, in an organization. It is not only a matter of organizational structure. Even the simplest examples we provided in Chapter 1 illustrate this fact. One aspect of this is physical proximity.

Many managers may already sense that physical proximity is conducive to communications and relations between groups and among individuals. Space allocation, though, is no panacea for ensuring the kinds of communication necessary in the innovation process. Communication is very complex, and the differences between and need for communication for coordination, information, and inspiration—the three types of communication we introduced in Chapter 2—have serious implications for the organizational structure questions that often determine physical space decisions in companies.

If a company's objective were to solidify the link between communication and innovation, it would be useful to know the degree to which physical space can be used to accomplish this goal. Recall that every activity has a social and a spatial dimension. Let's look at what we know about how physical space influences the formation and functioning of technical communication networks.

First, we know that proximity *does* have effects. People who work nearby come to know each other better, are much more likely to know and understand what each other is doing, and consequently are better equipped to coordinate their work. In terms of our communication types, they find *communication for coordination* relatively straightforward. Similarly, physical proximity to those with knowledge of developments inside or outside an organization increases your likelihood of keeping informed of those developments—supporting *communication for information.*

Managers, aware of the fact that proximity or the distance between worksites affects communication patterns and thus supports or hinders the goals of an organizational structure, tend to map physical locations to match that structure. That reinforces the intent of the organizational structure, but it may actually interfere with the innovation process by making *communication for inspiration* more difficult. In the network depicted in Figure 3-1, it's easy to conclude that something may be getting in the way of the communication between the two distinct groupings.

Figure 3-1 is very simple. It reveals only which individuals communicated with which other individuals—and that may be a function of the way the organization is structured. However, we are looking for evidence that the configuration of physical space may also play a role.

We know that all of the people in Figure 3-1 are in the same division of the company. They work in various departments that are expected to interact to a greater or lesser degree. To understand why they may or may not communicate, we need to take the analysis even further. A more advanced, specific method of measurement—the Netgraph—allows us to do so.

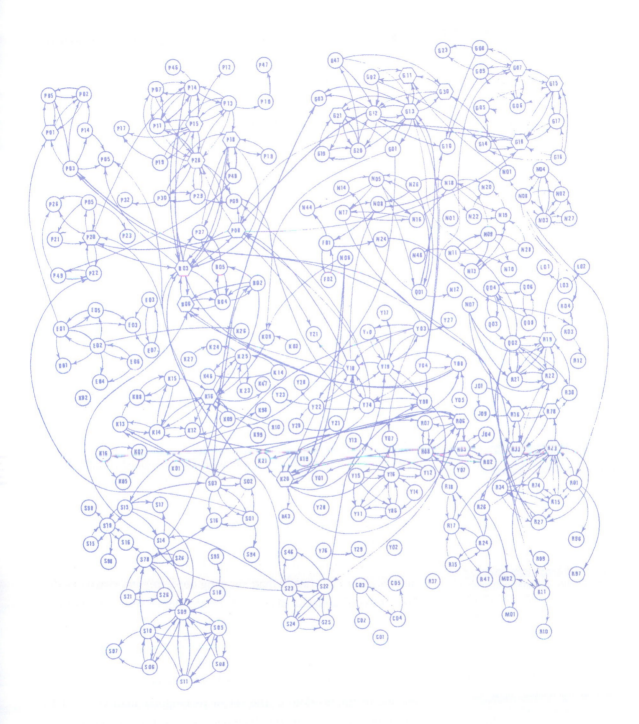

Figure 3-1 A simple map of an organization's communication network.

Netgraphs[1]: What They Are and How They Work

Communication networks can be represented graphically by their matrices—which is the basic approach of what we call "Netgraphing." In its most fundamental form, we convert an adjacency matrix to a graphic grid. On a large square lattice, Netgraphs record contacts wherever they appear in the matrix. The complete picture looks like a large square grid that is selectively filled to indicate contacts between two people. All individuals in a Netgraph are on both the x and y axes.

Netgraphs can be rearranged based on variables such as measures of physical or organizational location, different roles in the organizational structure, work on various projects, demographic information about individuals, and so on. Boundaries can be established within a Netgraph to delineate visually the different "values" of a given variable. Using color, the Netgraph can also be sorted to show characteristics among pairs of individuals, such as whether they are both managers or engineers or work on the same project team or whether they do not share these characteristics.

In sum, a Netgraph is a pictorial representation of networks that maintains the unit of analysis at the level of each individual while retaining comparative information with regard to all other relevant individuals.

The first Netgraph in Figure 3-2 shows a company division with three departments, which are sorted according to geography (i.e., where they are physically located). The thicker lines indicate that two departments are colocated within one building, but in different wings, and the third department is in a separate building. Every filled-in square indicates communication between two people, and the colors indicate whether this communication is intra- (purple, red, and blue) or interdepartmental (gray). It is clear that there is far more interdepartmental communication between individuals when located in the same building.

The Netgraph in Figure 3-3 sorts the data about these same three departments, now with the separate building shown in the center, in a different way. Around the departments shown in Figure 3-2, we now see in Figure 3-3 different levels of leadership, from the edge of the figure moving in toward the center. There are two levels of division leaders (in red) and then departmental managers (also in red, always shown adjacent to the teams they lead). The thin gray lines separate members of departments into the various projects on which they are working. Clusters of gray indicate communication across projects, while clusters of blue indicate communication within projects. It becomes apparent that the divisional leaders communicate with the department leaders and with individuals throughout the three departments, but that department leaders mostly limit their communication to within their own departments. It is still obvious that the department located in a separate building enjoys far less communication even with division leaders.

Finally, we come to the Netgraph in Figure 3-4, which sorts the same division but, rather than showing departments, visualizes the flow of work along the diagonal from the upper left to the bottom right. Purple clusters indicate groups of employees working together on a given task. Green indicates the communication between these clusters as they hand off their completed work to the next, adjacent group; black indicates communication between groups that is not specific to this workflow. The set of rectangular matrices next to the square matrices on the diagonal are indicators of the amount of contact between each pair of squares. Where there is little or no communication shown between adjacent groups, it turns out that

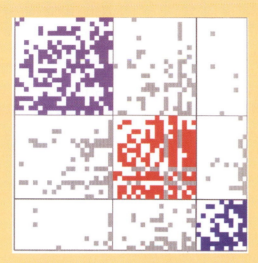

Figure 3-2 In this Netgraph, the rows and columns are sorted by geography—where people are physically located in the organization. The effect of physical location on communication can be clearly seen.

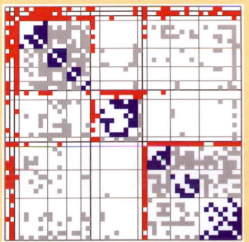

Figure 3-3 In this Netgraph, rows and columns are sorted according to the position of the individuals in the organizational hierarchy.

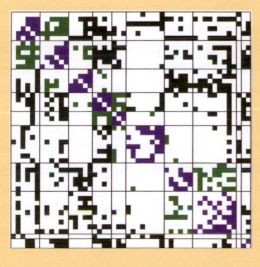

Figure 3-4 In this Netgraph, rows and columns are sorted according to the group position along the organization's workflow.

the physical separation of people in a separate building is the culprit. Any communication that doesn't happen in the exact order of the workflow still must happen, even if it means circumventing one party—which introduces major inefficiency to the workflow.

Similar situations occur frequently in the analyses. An analysis can be taken even further by measuring the walking distances between every pair of engineers or scientists in the organization and relating the distances to communication frequency. A curve can then be plotted that shows probability of communication declining with distance (Figure 3-5).[2] As it turns out, the probability that people in a given organization will communicate with each other declines precipitously the farther away from each other they are situated and reaches an asymptotic level at about 50 meters.

One very possible explanation for the curve in Figure 3-5 is that it is merely an artifact of the way in which people are located within facilities. Again, managers tend to locate together people who work together. Those people naturally tend to communicate more with one another than with others with whom they have no work relationship. This, however, suggests that it is still organizational structure at play, not distance or proximity.

The existence of a relationship based on working in the same department adds a constant to the probability of communication (Figure 3-6). Common departmental membership increases the likelihood of communication independent of separation distance. On the other hand, you are more likely to communicate with someone in your department who is also in the next office than with a departmental colleague in the next building.

Other factors affect communication among technical people in organizations. For instance, the probability that a pair of scientists or engineers will engage in frequent technical communication is a function of the degree to which they share a common base of knowledge, the rate at which that knowledge base is developing, the size of their department, the degree of interdependence in their work, and the distance between their workstations.

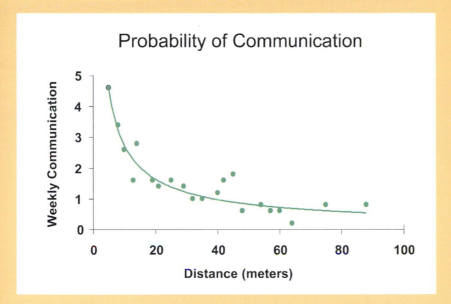

Figure 3-5 The probability of a pair of people in an organization communicating with each other declines rapidly as the distance between them increases.

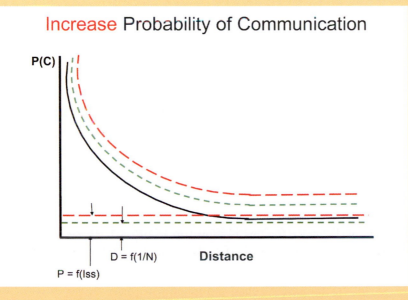

Figure 3-6 People who share membership in a department are more likely to communicate regularly. This effect is independent of the distance between them.

Readers may legitimately wonder whether this analysis of the effects of distance on face-to-face communication also applies to other communication media. After all, wasn't the telephone invented in part to resolve the problem of distance? And, therefore, shouldn't the probability of telephone communication increase as distance increases? It sounds reasonable to presume that the telephone substitutes for face-to-face communication. What about electronic mail? Will it not also function in this way?

We expected affirmative answers to these questions, but what we found is a bit different. For example, rather than finding that the probability of telephone communication increases with distance, as face-to-face probability decays, our data show a decay in the use of *all* communication media with distance (following a "near-field" rise). We should not have been surprised. Many studies have shown a decline in telecommunication with distance. Many studies have shown that most telephone calls from a household are to points within a short radius. Biksen and Eveland (1986) found a similar pattern for electronic mail.

One reason for the pattern observed in our data is that all of these media, as well as the written medium, are correlated in their use. We communicate with nearly the same people through all of these media. For example, we talk with the same people both by telephone and face-to-face. We also send e-mail messages and written memoranda to the same people. We do not keep separate sets of people, some of whom we communicate with by one medium and some by another. The more often we see someone face-to-face, the more likely it is that we will also telephone that person or communicate by another medium. Evidence for this is shown in Figure 3-7. These data are from a study in which Oscar Hauptman monitored the communication among the sites of a geographically dispersed computer manufacturer (Laboratory I) (Allen and Hauptman 1989).

When we relate the probability of face-to-face communication to that of telephone, we find nearly all of the points are on the diagonal. The probabilities are equal for most pairings of separate sites. The only exceptions are for sites that are near enough to allow more face-to-face contact. Had there been any substitution of telephone for face-to-face, points would have fallen in the upper-left quadrant. There are no points in that quadrant.

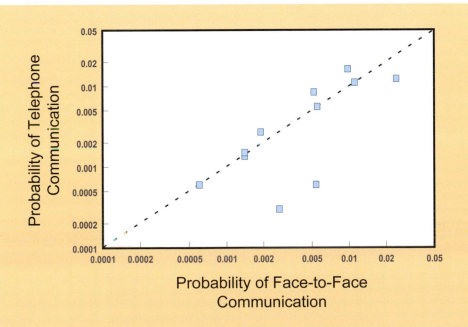

Figure 3-7 This plot shows how strongly correlated are the relationships between telephone and face-to-face communication between locations. The more frequently we talk with someone face-to-face, the more likely we are also to talk with that person by phone.

More important, perhaps, is the fact that telephone and electronic mail (at least in its present form) are what we might call "bandwidth limited." We mean this in more than just the physical sense. Discussing anything that is complex or abstract by telephone or electronic mail is very difficult. We need to meet directly with the person. We may phone or send an e-mail, but that is usually to arrange the meeting at which the real communication takes place. We call and say, "Will you be in this afternoon? I really have to come over and talk to you about something."

The evidence for this again comes from the Hauptman study. When asked to indicate the complexity of each communication as well as the medium, respondents evidenced a strong correlation between the two. Telephone was used for less complex communication (Figure 3-8), and face-to-face was used for more complex information (Figure 3-9).

Both observations are largely independent of the distance separating the communicating pair. The reasons for this are manifold. First, many things, particularly technical ideas and problems, are difficult to communicate with words alone. We need the assistance of diagrams or sketches. In addition, we often need the feedback that comes from looking into the other person's eyes, which communicate understanding. Anyone who has ever taught a class will testify to this. When that glazed appearance comes over the students' eyes, you know you've lost them.

Similarly, in describing an idea or technical problem to people, you can tell whether they are following you. Body language, particularly from the eyes, provides unspoken feedback that is very powerful. If the indication is negative, you are prompted to restate the information in a different way. This feedback system is invaluable in guiding communication. Telephone communication does not typically allow this feedback. Videoconferencing and some new forms of e-mail allow people to see one another, and this can be a very great help, but none of these forms yet provide the same broadband communication available in a direct encounter. Consequently, videoconferencing, at least thus far, provides insufficient resolution to afford the same precision in eye contact and the accompanying feedback available in a face-to-face encounter. Written communication and the most prevalent forms of electronic mail suffer the additional difficulty that they are asynchronous. Any feedback at all on understanding is delayed in time. Most videoconferencing suffers the additional drawback of being restricted to formally scheduled meetings. This is a help mainly for communication for coordination, the first of the three types of communication discussed earlier. The second and third types—communication for information and inspiration—are seldom conveyed through formal meetings.

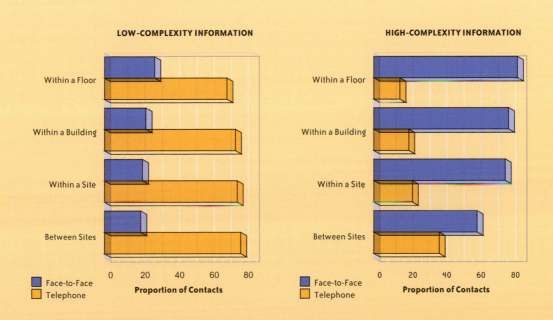

Figure 3-8 This plot shows communication medium as a function of distance for information of low complexity. The telephone is used extensively for communicating on simple topics, even when the distance is short.

Figure 3-9 This plot shows communication medium as a function of distance for information of high complexity. Face-to-face communication is used extensively for complex communication, even when the distance is extended.

The Role Played by Physical Space

What does this discussion of communication have to do with physical space? It's safe to say that the probability of frequent technical communication among engineers and scientists is determined by their locations in both physical and organizational space. And if communication is necessary for the innovation process—as we know it is—then where that physical space exists is going to matter quite a lot.

Getting people to talk with each other is the only truly effective way of transferring technical knowledge and advancing the process of innovation. Organizational boundaries are the biggest barrier to letting this happen because organizational boundaries separate cultures and the ways people think and do things. They also separate the people whose brains are the vessels carrying the knowledge that must be combined for innovation.

Innovative ideas seldom come full blown from a single source, but from a variety of sources. An organization succeeds with innovation when it makes it possible to share information and then integrate knowledge into what becomes the innovative idea.

In our experience, even when organizations *do* think about these issues, they give little or no consideration to the role played by physical space and space configuration in the innovation process.

Often, people are *not* communicating, even though they work in an organization structured such that there ought to be a high degree of interaction with others in their group or department. The only way to determine why is to go to the site and look around. We find things like this: A department ran out of space in the building and "temporarily" sent three staff members out to a trailer in the parking lot. Or we find that space was available in the next building, only 20 meters across a driveway. Or we learn that the department's second-floor space was getting too crowded, so a few staff members were sent to a less-cramped space on the fifth floor. That was six months ago, and no one since has gone up to see whether they're still around.

The organization might as well have sent the staff to another country as to another building. As for sending them "only" a few floors up, they might as well have been launched into outer space.

We see this scenario time and again: The particular shape of a communication network within an organization results very heavily from the *physical location* of the people and the structure of the *physical space.* The scale of the problem is quite revealing. As Figure 3-5 shows, a mere 50 meters' separation between people essentially results in the end of regular communication.

What can be done to thwart the problem of separation? A straightforward solution is to acknowledge that 50 meters' separation is a major problem and then work to overcome it. A simple application of this idea is the placement of a coffee pot, a conference room, or shared instrumentation.

The Danger of Managers Generalizing from Their Own Behavior

Managers may be tempted to generalize about the use of different communication media based on their own behavior, but this constitutes a serious danger. Managers communicate by telephone far more than do engineers and scientists, and hence they tend to believe that the telephone (or e-mail) will work as well for the engineers as it does for them. "Why do they need to travel?" managers often ask about engineers and scientists.

Managers must remember that, on average, they deal with less complex information than do the engineers and scientists reporting to them. Compared with technical information, a much greater proportion of management information can be communicated by telephone.

When we distinguish between managers and engineers or scientists and between telephone and face-to-face communication by plotting separate networks, the managers stand out as telephone users, whereas engineers and scientists communicate face-to-face. Notably, when managers face a complex issue, they too recognize the need to meet with the other parties in the same room.

Let's delve a bit deeper into the nature and sensitivity of the bonds resulting from physical proximity or common organizational membership. For a number of organizations we've studied, we have computed from our data the probabilities of communication under varying degrees of physical and organizational separation. The results of one such computation are shown in Table 3-1, where we vary physical separation along the vertical axis and organizational separation along the horizontal.[3] The probability of communication for those most remote from each other is shown in the lower left and that for those most proximate is in the upper right. Immediately, we see the sensitivity of communication to physical separation. Unless engineers and scientists are very close to one another, there is very little likelihood of regular communication. The second thing to notice is that different types of organizational membership differ in the strength of their effect. Being assigned to the same project team has a generally stronger effect than does sharing membership in a department.

When engineers are housed in the same wing of a building, we see—for the first time—some reasonable probability that those with no organizational relation will communicate regularly, at least in Laboratory H (Table 3-2). In other words, it is only once this degree of proximity is reached that inspirational communication has any chance of occurring. To encourage this creativity-stimulating communication, management must create situations in which chance encounters will occur. People seldom, if ever, actively seek inspirational communication. For it to happen, people must either be housed very near to each other or must share the use of some facility that brings them into occasional contact.

One of the more surprising results of our research is the low value for communication probability between wings on the same floor of traditional buildings. When there is no organizational relationship between the people in separate wings, the probability that they will communicate regularly decreases by as much as 75 percent from what it would be were they located in the same wing (Table 3-3). Of course, the way in which the buildings are configured influences this. In both Laboratory H and Laboratory I, narrow hallways with some offices connect the wings, with most people housed in the two wings.

TABLE 3-1 The Effects of Physical and Organizational Separation as Measured in One Organization

	Different Departments and Projects	*Same Department, Different Project*	*Same Project, Different Departments*	*Same Department and Project*
Same Wing	0.16	0.69	0.71	0.95
Same Floor, Different Wings	0.05	0.53	0.80	*
Same Building, Different Floors	0.05	0.35	*	*
Same Site, Different Buildings	0.02	0.60	0.33	0.50
Different Sites	0.002	0.15	0.23	0.38

*Too few observations.

Reversals in probability in columns 2 and 3 are probably due to noisy data.

TABLE 3-2 Organizational Relationships and Probability of Technical Communication within a Wing

Organizational Relationship	Laboratory H	Laboratory I
Different Departments and Projects	0.16	0.08
Shared Department but Different Projects	0.69	0.19
Shared Project but Different Departments	0.71	*
Both Department and Project Shared	0.95	0.42

*Data not available.

TABLE 3-3 Organizational Relationships and Probability of Technical Communication between Wings (or the same floor) of a Building

Organizational Relationship	Laboratory H	Laboratory I
Different Departments and Projects	0.06	0.05
Shared Department but Different Projects	0.53	0.09
Shared Project but Different Departments	0.80	*
Both Department and Project Shared	*	0.29

*Too few observations.

When there is an organizational relationship between people in the separate wings, communication increases dramatically, as shown in Table 3-3. There is an order-of-magnitude increase in the probability of regular communication. Dividing a project between wings had virtually no effect on communication among team members in Laboratory H.

When engineers are in the same building but on separate floors and with no organizational relationship, there is very little chance they will communicate regularly (Table 3-4). They might as well be in separate buildings. Floors have a way of capturing people. We seldom think of the other floors when we are in a multistory building. The other floors are usually out of sight, and the building, in our minds, might as well be only the floor we can see.

In Laboratory H, the existence of a departmental relationship substantially increases the probability that people will travel between floors. In Laboratory I, there is some increased probability—but not nearly as much. Organizational relationships have much less effect on communication among the software engineers in Laboratory I.[4]

TABLE 3-4 **Organizational Relationships and Probability of Weekly Technical Communication between Floors of a Building**

Organizational	Laboratory H	Laboratory I
Different Departments and Projects	0.05	0.01
Shared Department but Different Projects	0.60	0.06
Shared Project but Different Departments*	*	*
Both Department and Project Shared*	—	*

*Too few observations.

Now, of what value are tables of this sort? Let's assume that you are responsible for managing two departments at two locations—in other words, two departments that are physically separated in some way. This separation could be in the form of separate wings on the same floor of a building, or it could be separate floors in a building, separate buildings, or separate sites on different continents. The situation is similar to that shown in Figure 3-10.

To reduce the mean level of physical separation, you might transfer some people between the two departments (Figure 3-11). Now the two transferred subunits are in closer proximity to the remaining members of the original separate departments. Being closer will increase the probability of communication among these pairs of individuals.

Before we proceed thinking that we have solved the problem, we must realize that there is a downside to this simple solution. It is now less likely that the transferred individuals will communicate as frequently with their departmental colleagues. Nothing comes without a price.

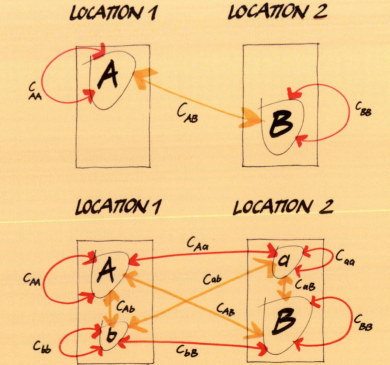

Figure 3-10 The combination of both a physical and an organizational separation between two departments reduces communication between the two departments drastically.

Figure 3-11 Transferring people between two departments, even departments that are physically separated, introduces physical bonds to offset the organizational separation and leaves organizational bonds that partially offset the newly introduced physical separation.

In Figure 3-12, we see what would have happened in Laboratory I had we transferred engineers between floors in one of their buildings. We calculated the effect on communication probability of moving different proportions of staff. As you can see, in this case, giving up about 15 percent of internal communication results in a more than twofold increase in interdepartmental communication. Of course, the reason that the cost is so little compared with the gain is that there remains an organizational bond between A and a (and between b and B) to overcome the physical separation we have imposed. The twofold gain is due to the fact that there is now physical proximity between a and B and between b and A where there was formerly neither physical nor organizational propinquity.

Using the figures from Laboratory H and weighting them by the number of pairs of people in different circumstances, it is easy to calculate the function shown in Figure 3-12. Beginning with each department on its own floor (no one transferred), we can see that the probability of regular intradepartmental communication is high, and the probability of communication between staff in the separate departments is very low.

Transferring 10 percent of the staff between the two floors more than doubles the probability of interdepartmental communication but is paid for by a 15 percent decrease in probability of intradepartmental communication. As the proportion of transferred staff increases, the probability of regular communication between the departments increases accordingly. At the same time, the probability of internal communication decreases. This continues until the departments are evenly divided between the floors. At this point, the probability of regular technical communication between the departments has quadrupled. Internal communication has been decreased by about 40 percent to pay for this.

There is no optimum point on the Figure 3-12 curve. It merely shows the nature of the trade-off. The manager must decide the relative value of the directions for communication. The curve shows what it will cost, in terms of internal communication, to gain increased contact with another part of the organization.[5]

While the analysis above illustrates our point, it is important to remember that the numbers are by no means definitive. The two organizations from which data are drawn differ in many respects, as reflected in the large differences in the probability of their staff members communicating regularly under different circumstances. When people are grouped together physically in Laboratory I, the effect on communication is much weaker than in H. Between any two organizations, sites are not always laid out in the same way; buildings are configured in many ways; even the separation between floors can be quite different from building to building. A given building in one organization, for example, might have an atrium affording visual contact between floors, whereas a similar building in another might not have a feature that allows such visual contact—and thus moving people between floors will have less effect in the former case than in the latter. In the comparison here, Laboratory I's buildings are much larger than are those of H. The floors and wings are correspondingly larger. Furthermore, even the definition of "site" differs dramatically. Laboratory H has six locations, each with a campus-type array of buildings, whereas I locates its buildings in city centers. There were never more than two buildings at any one site. Therefore, what may appear to be equivalent proximities may, in fact, be very different. In addition, the same terms for organizational structure may not have the same meaning in different organizations. Departments are much larger in Laboratory I than they are in H. Projects were also generally larger, with probably less average interdependence. There are also great differences in the nature of the technologies in which the two organizations are engaged. This has a profound effect on the need for communication.[6]

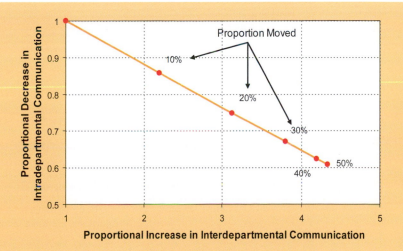

Figure 3-12 The Trade-off between Inter- and Intradepartmental Communication as Staff Are Divided between Two Floors of a Building (Laboratory H)

Beyond the general points of this analysis, separate calculations must be made for other organizations. An example of the need for separate calculation for communication between two sites is shown in Figure 3-13, again using Laboratories H and I.

This analysis is oversimplified and relatively conservative, since it does not take into account anything beyond direct contact between individuals; that is, it ignores the fact that those individuals can make referrals to other individuals. A transferred individual will often make the remark, "That is an interesting problem. Did you know that Person B, over in my department, was working on something like that last year?" As a result, the transfer of people between physical locations can, in reality, have a much greater effect than shown in the figures above.

What do we learn from all of these analyses? It is no surprise that engineers separated physically are unlikely to communicate frequently. What the analyses show, however, is that an effective way to overcome this communication problem is to have at least some people at the two locations share an organizational bond.[7]

Nevertheless, we do know that organizational structure interacts with physical layout to determine communication patterns. In addition, we now know a little more about the relative strength of this interaction for varying forms of organization and different degrees of physical separation. Let's now look at some examples of buildings where physical space and organizational structure were at least considered together.

Figure 3-13 Moving Staff between Sites to Increase Interdepartmental Communication (Examples from Laboratories H and I)

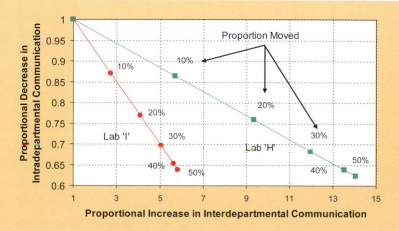

The Configuration of Physical Space May Hinder Interaction

It doesn't take too onerous a search to find examples of buildings that seem to have been designed to hinder the interaction of those who inhabit the space. Of course, there may be occasional instances in which this is a good thing. But there are also some specific things that can be done that, it turns out, are *very* important to incorporate, as well as some to avoid. What follows is meant to illustrate and reinforce our contention that there is an intimate connection between physical space and communication, physical space and awareness, and physical space and the innovation process in an organization.

First, it seems obvious that an organization that wants its technical staff members to communicate needs to ensure the distances among them are minimized. Unfortunately, the traditional and most common form of office configuration does just the opposite. We saw this in the "before" and "after" illustrations of the European manufacturing company in Chapter 1 (Figures 1-3 and 1-4). That was the situation that faced the senior management: offices strung one after the other, in a linear fashion, along a corridor. At least these executives shared a corridor. In many buildings, those who need to communicate have far greater physical separation.

What is the solution, then, if the goal is to minimize separation distances? From a completely theoretical point of view, one could argue that the circle does that—but how many buildings have sites for which a circle works? A square is more conventional, and to minimize separation, it appears that a square, single-story building might be the most desirable. We say single-story because the evidence indicates that vertical separation always has a more severe effect than an equivalent amount of horizontal separation (but the difference hasn't been quantified because too much depends upon the nature of the vertical connections).

All of this is intended to illustrate how important it is simply to give *consideration* to the issue of physical space configuration in the innovation process. In no way do we mean through these simple points to trivialize the complexity of designing a building.

Taking Physical Space Configuration to the Extreme

Sometimes, the linear arrangement can be taken to an extreme that has an even worse effect on communication than is typically the case. Consider the design plans for a new laboratory in Figure 3-14, in the form of two connected letter *L*s, one inverted. Of course, such a building would be disastrous, with an extremely low probability of communication between the two distant wings. In fact, it is doubtful that those housed at the end of one wing would even be aware of the existence of the other wing.

Why would such a building be created? In this case, the answer is quite straightforward. First, there was a lakeshore along which the building would be contoured. That determined the general shape. The company also insisted that each occupant of the building have an office with a window looking out. This was easily accommodated with a linear form.

This sort of building would have been a disaster for the organization (which was highly dependent upon good internal technical communication). Fortunately, it was stopped in time—but that is not always the case. Many organizations have R&D facilities that are as bad or worse.

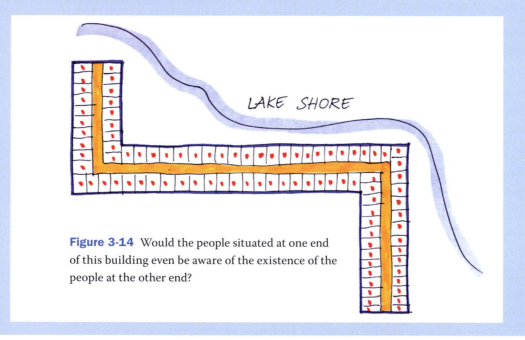

Figure 3-14 Would the people situated at one end of this building even be aware of the existence of the people at the other end?

Nevertheless, we'll posit that overcoming vertical separation matters. It can be done with wide-open, brightly lit, accessible staircases; some buildings have very dimly lit corner stairs with heavy steel fire doors. Others have reliable elevators. Or, as in retail stores, there might be escalators. Retail stores proved our point a long time ago, and while we again do not intend to suggest specific aspects of building design, retailers found escalators to be the best way to make the customer *aware* that there are other floors and goods on those floors. The significant cost of an escalator, reasons the retailer, is more than offset by the benefits.

Let's consider this in the context of *communication for inspiration*, which we indicated earlier is as likely to happen through chance or impromptu encounters as in any other way. Imagine extending the idea of the department store to an R&D laboratory and enabling what might be called "people browsing." It would be highly desirable if the unanticipated, impromptu encounters are the ones that often produce the most creative ideas. Open movement between floors, with "people browsing" along the way, creates conditions in which this type of communication is more likely to occur.

We've talked about distance and vertical separation. Another important element in stimulating communication is visual contact in real time. Qualitative observations lead us to conclude that people need to be prompted occasionally and reminded of the existence of potential technical communication partners. This holds true for all three types of communication—for coordination, information, and inspiration.

In the first instance, coordination, visual contact might remind an engineer that he needs to tell the person he sees about a design change. In terms of communication for information, visual contact could be a reminder that a certain person is the "resident expert" to go to with a given question. It is in the realm of communication for inspiration—the communication that stimulates creativity and the creation of new knowledge—that visual contact is probably most important. If people do not see one another, they will not have the opportunity to interact and create that knowledge.

What does all of this have to do with vertical separation? One of the major barriers to visual contact in a building is the separation of floors. In most buildings, each floor is visually isolated. When we exit the elevator on a given floor of a building, we quickly forget about the existence of the other floors. There is a tendency for our mental image of the building to be limited to a single floor—the floor on which we happen to be. Communication demands that we be reminded not only that there are other floors, but also that there are people working on those floors.

Vertical Separation in the Sears Tower

Sears, Roebuck & Co. occupied the Sears Tower in Chicago when construction was completed in 1973. At the time, it was the world's tallest building. In 1993, Sears began moving its offices out of the Tower and had completely vacated the building by 1995 in favor of an office "campus" in a Chicago suburb. Part of the reason was the huge financial burden of the building; Sears had been forced to take out a mortgage because of low occupancy. But some of the other motivations speak to the points we are making. The vertical separation of the Tower inhibited communication between different departments —something Sears missed from earlier days, when it occupied low-rise buildings on Chicago's West Side. In the Tower, Sears had as many cultures as it occupied floors. Vertical separation made the building a hindrance to the company.

The Steelcase Example

Let's return to a building example that offers an opportunity to explore whether the configuration of physical space can, in fact, affect communication positively. The building is the Steelcase Corporate Development Center in Gaines Township, Michigan. We use this building because the *intention* behind the physical space configuration illustrates our points.

Steelcase, a company that specializes in office environments, decided in the late 1980s to construct this building to house its principal functional departments involved in innovation: R&D, product engineering, industrial design, manufacturing engineering, marketing, purchasing, and corporate communications. A fairly large building was required—in fact, more than 60,000 square meters to house departments that had been spread among several buildings located at three sites in the Grand Rapids metropolitan area. Steelcase wanted to bring these departments together to improve their interdepartmental communication, shorten what was considered to be excessive product development time, and enhance innovation.

Senior management attributed the product development problem in large part to the organizational structure. Individual departments carried responsibility for given projects for a period that corresponded to a "stage" in the process and, only upon completion of their work, would pass the project along to the next department. The company hoped a new building would support a change in project management so that all involved in a given product development would communicate more effectively.

There were several assumptions underlying the building project, including that "innovative product solutions require enormous amounts of information about technology, design, the production process, and the market to be widely shared at all stages of the development process." Further, the company believed it crucial that there be "informal communication across project teams and across disciplines to stimulate creativity" (Becker 1990, p. 236).[8] By locating all the functions together, senior management expected closer interdepartmental contact, interaction, and relationships.

The building would need to be several stories high. To reduce the isolation of one floor from another, an atrium was constructed in the center of the building. An atrium can be an effective way of providing visual contact between floors in a building, particularly if it is centrally located. It enables people to see across to other floors as well as their own. This reminder of the existence of other floors, and of the people housed there, helps overcome the typical isolation of one floor from another. In fact, it increases the probability of communication by an order of magnitude, as is revealed by the example of Corning's Decker Building later in this chapter (and specifically in Table 3-8, on page 81).

The Steelcase building has a square footprint, and the atrium is approximately 21 meters square directly in the center (Figure 3-15). It begins at the entry floor and continues to the third floor, at which point it is divided into four triangular atria by a centralized cluster of offices, occupied by the heads of the departments. The atrium provides visual contact between floors near the center of the building. To provide visual contact between floors, at the perimeter, the outer walls lean back and form a pyramid, as Figure 3-16 shows.

Figure 3-15 The atrium of the Steelcase building provides visual contact between floors at the building's center.

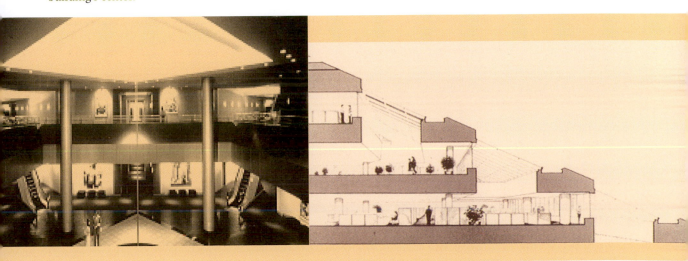

Figure 3-16 The outer walls of the Steelcase building form a pyramid that allows visual contact between floors at the building's perimeter.

While the physical space was intended to stimulate communication among its occupants, Steelcase went even further to combine the two tools of organizational structure and physical space to achieve its objectives. The company structured a *matrix* by using both physical and organizational location. Existing functional departments, which had strong structures and identities, were retained. But rather than locating departments together in the traditional way, management created "neighborhoods" of people from all the functions working in given product areas. In other words, physical space in the new building was allocated not departmentally but to these product areas, with people in the "neighborhoods" physically located without regard for their particular departmental affiliation, although they retained their normal reporting relationships (which were reinforced by regular departmental meetings). The result was a matrix hybrid with physical and organizational characteristics. The departmental side of the matrix and the connection to the knowledge base was maintained; the product line side of the matrix was established through the physical proximity of all those working in a given product area.

TABLE 3-5 Strength of the Communication Bonds Among the Six* Functional Departments before and after Moving into the New Building

Department	Product Engineering		Manufacturing Engineering		Marketing		Industrial		Purchasing	
	Before	After	Before	After	Before	After	Before	After	Before	After
Research and Development	30.80	29.00	9.70	8.90	0	20.40	22.20	71.40	0	10.20
Product Engineering			24.80	32.60	16.80	21.10	42.70	60.40	22.00	20.70
Manufacturing Engineering					12.10	30.40	14.30	62.50	11.50	13.40
Marketing							24.30	71.40	0	6.10
Industrial Design									39.70	35.70

* One department (Corporate Communications!) returned too few responses to be included in the analysis.

Interdepartmental communication among knowledge workers in the new building definitely increased. We sampled communication for 15 weeks in the old facilities and for 15 weeks in the new building. Taking the number of possible pairings of individuals in any two departments and dividing that into the number of pairs who actually communicate (weekly) provides a good indicator of the amount of communication between two departments.[9] In Table 3-5, we show the general increase in communication. The overall effect on interdepartmental communication is certainly positive.

Clearly, as we show in Table 3-6, this increase in *inter*departmental communication did not cost the company communication *within* the departments. In fact, the increase in interdepartmental communication was surpassed by the increase in *intra*department communication. Only one department registered a decrease. The combined use of organizational structure and physical space as management tools appears to have worked to maintain and strengthen intradepartmental communication—*despite* the fact that each department had its members spread around in the different product area "neighborhoods." The data show that the effects of vertical separation can be overcome.

TABLE 3-6 **Strength of Communication Bonds within the Functional Departments before and after the Move into the New Building**

Department	Before	After	Difference
Research and Development	60.00	66.67	6.67
Product Engineering	16.06	11.17	−4.89
Manufacturing Engineering	18.06	35.00	16.94
Marketing	22.78	22.86	0.08
Industrial Design	38.89	46.67	7.78
Purchasing	40.66	50.55	9.89

Where Should People Sit?

We've discussed vertical separation and proximity in the context of communication and awareness. Our discussion begs the questions of who ought to sit where and who ought to be located next to whom. We'll answer these questions here only in the context of one specific challenge: ensuring the opportunity for communication for inspiration, which is often given the least, if any, attention in making such decisions.

What if location decisions were made on the basis of whether creative results would be expected if two groups (or individuals) were to communicate (see Table 3-7)? It would, of course, be a subjective estimate, but managers make subjective estimates all the time. "If only we could get B to talk with D, something might result!" is usually followed with, "But they work in such different areas that we can't get them together." An optimal innovation process demands a different answer.

Communication for coordination suffers least as a result of physical separation, because the *need* to coordinate work will force communication even over substantial distances. Communication for inspiration is the most affected by separation, and it requires that people come into contact with each other. We've found that "chance encounters"—unplanned encounters between smart people with good ideas—often lead to innovative outcomes. The configuration of physical space in general, as well as the specific location of workstations, traffic patterns, and visibility will all increase the likelihood that chance encounters will occur.[10]

TABLE 3-7 **Determining Adjacencies**

		Work Independence	Potential for Creativity
Engineer 'A'			
	Engineer 'B'	HIGH	HIGH
	Engineer 'C'	LOW	HIGH
	Engineer 'B'	LOW	LOW
	Engineer 'D'	HIGH	LOW
	etc.		
Engineer 'B'			
	Engineer 'C'	HIGH	LOW
	Engineer 'D'	LOW	HIGH
	etc.		

* If these people aren't near, they won't communicate and potential for creativity will be lost.

The example of the Steelcase building suggests strongly that structuring and managing a product development organization is more than a question of organizational structure. After all, the matrix organizational structure the company adopted only went so far. What occurred in that matrix was heavily affected by the physical space in which people worked. While every manager knows that simple physical proximity is conducive to communications and relationships between groups and among individuals, the Steelcase example shows something far more: that the way physical space is configured can enhance the innovation process.

Steelcase did something else worth mentioning in its new building. As in the example of the European manufacturing company introduced in Chapter 1, the company clustered its senior managers around an open area. Previously, there had been quite limited contact among these individuals, who had been housed in separate buildings. The clustering aimed at breaking down Steelcase's silos, and putting the senior managers not at the top of the pyramid-shaped building but rather on a middle floor helped promote awareness. Management could see all the floors of the building where different parts of the organizational matrix were at work, and management could be seen by everyone.

The Corning Example

Another example of using the configuration of physical space to enhance communication and the innovation process is the Decker Building constructed by Corning Glass Works to house its Manufacturing Engineering organization (Figure 3-17). Driven by restrictions on the availability of land, the plan at the most desirable site was for a three-story building—which posed difficulties for communication, as we've shown.

One recommendation was to make it as easy as possible to travel between floors, perhaps with readily accessible staircases, elevators and, if the budget would permit, escalators as a way to do this. Another was to provide some visual contact between floors. Again, the option chosen was an atrium—opening as a triangle in the front of the building, continuing down the entire length of the building's middle, and re-opening as a triangle in the rear (Figure 3-18).

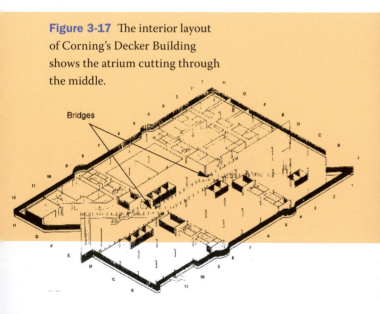

Figure 3-17 The interior layout of Corning's Decker Building shows the atrium cutting through the middle.

Bridges

Figure 3-18 The atrium of Corning's Decker Building provides visual contact between the floors.

From almost any point on any floor in this building, you can see some part of the other floors. Those who work in the building are constantly reminded of the existence of work areas other than their own. Most of the workstations on each floor are of the office landscape variety, with a combination of low and high panels. The enclosed offices seen in Figure 3-17 have glass walls front and back so they do not obstruct the view through to the atrium. Curtains can be drawn for privacy, but the norm is to leave them open. In addition to the atrium, which provides visual reminders of the other floors, there is provision for easy travel between floors. There are elevators toward the front and rear of the building (the cylindrical shapes in Figure 3-18), an open stairway and ramp rising from the reception area, and escalators in the front and rear.

Has all of this been effective? While it was impossible to sample communication before the organization moved into the building, we were able to do so after occupancy. In Table 3-8, which compares the probability of regular weekly technical communication between adjacent floors in the Decker Building with that computed for the two laboratories discussed earlier (without atria), we show a markedly higher value for the newer facility.

Of course, there are many other differences between organizations. We have no control over work relationships or any other form of relation that might exist between floors in the three organizations. Nevertheless, a difference of the magnitude shown in Table 3-8 leads one to suspect—*at least*—that allowing for visual contact and easy vertical movement certainly did no harm. There is also anecdotal evidence of a benefit. Occupants report occasions of seeing someone on a different floor and being reminded of something that they wanted to discuss with that person. An internal company study indicated a 15 percent improvement in productivity comparing the design of two very similar plants, before and after occupancy of the Decker Building.

Decker and Steelcase are relatively simple examples that illustrate some of our main points. In Chapters 4 and 5, we delve deeper into the role played by physical space as a management tool used in conjunction with how an organization is structured. Our discussion begins in Chapter 4 with an extended look at the importance

TABLE 3-8 Probability of Weekly Technical Communication Between Engineers on Separate Floors of a Building

Organization	P[C]
Laboratory H	0.01
Laboratory I	0.04
Corning's Decker Building	0.14

of awareness and the concept of centers of gravity within organizational structures and physical space configuration.

Notes

[1] This technique for representing a communication network was developed by Varghese George (now on the faculty of the University of Massachusetts) with a team of students at MIT.

[2] The communication frequency chosen when plotting Figure 3-5 is once a week or more. Had we chosen a less frequent level of communication, say once a month, the probability would not have declined quite as precipitously. We chose once a week as a measure of reasonably consistent communication.

[3] The probabilities shown in Table 3-1 are valid only for the given organization. A separate calculation has to be made for any other organization.

[4] There were too few projects with staff on separate floors in either organization (three pairs in Laboratory H and none in Laboratory I) to permit a calculation of the effect of project membership on communication probability.

[5] The relationship is independent of department size.

[6] This does not invalidate the analytic approach used here. It simply means that the numbers used are not universally applicable. Appropriate values must be generated for each situation. Such numbers are highly dependent upon the nature of the facility, the structure of the organization, and the nature of the work being performed.

[7] As was stated earlier, the probabilities reported here are fine for illustrating our point. They will not apply beyond the two organizations at hand. Comparable figures could be computed for other organizations, from which similar analyses could be undertaken.

[8] Becker (1990, pp. 236–238) described the competing project management approaches in the preceding paragraph as the "relay race" and the "rugby game," respectively.

[9] Some caveats are in order. During the study period, most of the department directors changed. Many other personnel also changed. The internal structuring of departments changed. A major project was completed, and so on. All of these factors could, and probably did, affect interdepartmental communication. Nevertheless, the formula from which the table is derived is as follows:

$$C_{ij} = 100\, n_{ij} / N_i N_j$$

where: n_{ij} = the number of pairs, who communicate at least once per week

N_i = the number of responding individuals in department i

N_j = the number of responding individuals in department j

[10]   A caveat is in order, though. It is decidedly *not* the case that physical proximity will *always* produce increased communication. We do not propose that new, well-designed buildings are always the answer to the dilemma organizations face.

References

Allen TJ, and Hauptman O (1989). The influence of communication technologies on organization structure: A framework for future research. *Communication Research* 14(5):575–587.

Becker F (1990). *The total workplace: Facilities management and the elastic organization*. New York: Van Nostrand Reinhold.

Biksen TK, and Eveland JD (1986). *New office technology: Planning for people*. New York: Pergamon Press.

4 Increasing Awareness

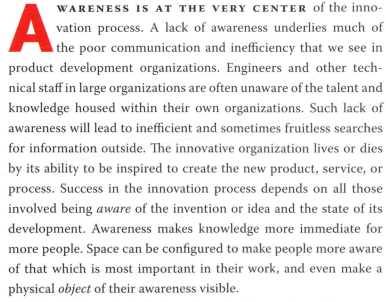

AWARENESS IS AT THE VERY CENTER of the innovation process. A lack of awareness underlies much of the poor communication and inefficiency that we see in product development organizations. Engineers and other technical staff in large organizations are often unaware of the talent and knowledge housed within their own organizations. Such lack of awareness will lead to inefficient and sometimes fruitless searches for information outside. The innovative organization lives or dies by its ability to be inspired to create the new product, service, or process. Success in the innovation process depends on all those involved being *aware* of the invention or idea and the state of its development. Awareness makes knowledge more immediate for more people. Space can be configured to make people more aware of that which is most important in their work, and even make a physical *object* of their awareness visible.

Awareness can be built through study, observation, and communication. The latter includes the exchange of thoughts, messages, or information through speech, signals, writing, or behavior. In the context of today's multidisciplinary product development organization, it is communication that builds awareness. In earlier research, we found that 80 percent of the information underlying new ideas

85

came about through personal communication (Allen 1984). Of such communication, that which produced the best ideas was with colleagues in an individual's own organization.

Communication necessarily involves some type of interaction. If awareness depends to some degree on communication, then it also depends on interaction. It should already be clear that communication is critically important when more than one person is involved in something. Successful communication can be the difference between meeting objectives and utter failure.

The spatial arrangements in which people work have an enormous effect on the degree to which they are aware of one another, what they are working on, and—to a degree—what they know about. Furthermore, of the three types of technical communication that we are considering, communication for inspiration is the type most affected by physical space. Most communication of this type occurs during *chance encounters*, which create the possibility for inspiration and creativity—the sources of innovation. It is very obvious that the ways in which physical space is configured can strongly promote or impede the occurrence of chance encounters.

As we showed in Chapter 2, certain stages of the innovation process demand far more attention to physical space than do others. This goes well beyond making an effort to locate people who work together near to each other. A far more comprehensive approach is required that promotes many different types of communication and thus promotes awareness.

The *potential* for and *need* for awareness in today's organization are greater than ever before. Far greater numbers of people can be empowered to make their own decisions, find their own innovative paths, and serve the broader interests of the organization in doing so. The affordability of advanced communication technology now allows any size organization to realize both the benefits of economies of scale and knowledge that were once restricted mostly to larger organizations and the creativity and flexibility that are more typically motivated in smaller groups. To capture these benefits, Thomas Malone, for example, argued that organizations are becoming increasingly *decentralized* as people make their own decisions (Malone 2004).

Changing Organizational Patterns

Communication evolved over time to get us to the point of decentralization, describes Thomas Malone. As he explains, communication was once limited to face-to-face communication among small groups of 15 to 50 individuals. After a long period of decentralized individuals or small groups, larger societies with "central rulers" were organized. Inevitably, as population density grew and centralized, hierarchical forms of organization emerged.

New communication systems, established to support centralized decision making, mirrored these hierarchical forms of organization. Writing, in particular, allowed for communication over long distances without ever needing to meet face-to-face. And the invention of the printing press reduced the cost of communicating within large groups, beginning what Malone calls a "democratic revolution" as people became better informed.

Eventually, technology—the typewriter, telephone, and so on—made communication even easier and less costly, helping to spur larger and larger organizations. Nevertheless, the hierarchical form of organization persisted. Even newer technologies—such as e-mail—later emerged to facilitate a change to the *decentralized* form of organization.

In Figure 4-1, we see this evolution. We represent the centralized, hierarchical form of organization in the figure with a typical organizational chart. Person A's communication with Person B is indirect and must follow a circuitous path. But with decentralization, they are able to communicate as part of a network. Through the configuration of physical space, it could be easy for them to interact with Person C, who might even be on a different level and even a different "side" of the typical organizational chart, creating the possibility for communication that might not otherwise have happened, or at least making it more likely in real time.

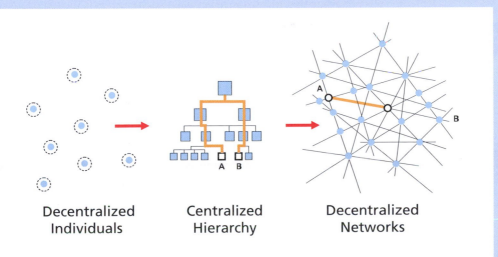

Decentralized Individuals   Centralized Hierarchy   Decentralized Networks

Figure 4-1 Changing patterns of organization affect how people communicate. Centralized hierarchies formed over time by decentralized individuals have now evolved, and more decentralized networks allow for direct communication between people.

This change in organizational patterns has the potential to enhance opportunities for collaboration and eliminate barriers prevalent in a hierarchy, thus increasing interaction and awareness. It also is related to the concept of centers of gravity, which we next discuss.

Centers of Gravity and Awareness

The previous discussion focused on the changes that have taken place in the ways people might be situated in an organizational structure. Of course, how people spend their time at work is also an important determinant of communication. Few people remain in their individual workspaces all day; most distribute their time among a variety of locations over the course of a day. Depending on assignments, time might be spent in laboratories, the local plant, coffee areas, and certainly conference rooms. Therefore, the existence of and access to these areas are important. In fact, if we could take each location in a given physical space, measure how much time people spend there, and then weight it according to the proportion of time, we could compute a center of gravity for each individual. We could then argue that the distance between such centers is the true determinant of communication likelihood, more so than the distance between workstations. This would help illustrate the centrality of physical space and challenge some of the conventional wisdom about space—for instance, the notion that you can't shift people's centers of gravity without changing their office locations.

We know from this definition of centers that they can be shifted without changing the location of anyone's workstation. If each group in an organization is colocated around its own conference room, group members have little incentive to leave their immediate area. For example, physical space with shared conference rooms, all located in the same part of a building, might be substituted for every subgroup within an organization having its own conference room. Centralizing conference rooms means that people will have to travel to them; this would have a profound influence on traffic patterns and on the possibility that people who rarely communicate might run into each other and interact. If, while you are on your way to a meeting, you pass by a colleague's office, your separation distance is much shorter and you are relatively high on the probability axis of Figure 3-5 in Chapter 3. Centers of gravity would be shifted.

The location of offices, labs, coffee pots, conference rooms, and so on can be arranged to influence the movement of people in directions that will create desired communication patterns. Of course, we usually need a reason to talk to others beyond social niceties. But how often do we have something in mind we might like to discuss with someone else but don't because we remain in our offices or in our immediate areas? If we happen to be passing near the right person's office, we're likely to stop in.

Communication for *inspiration*—the type of communication that leads to creativity—often results from people interacting with those with whom they do not usually come into contact. Perhaps they work in different disciplines, on different projects, or in different product areas. They run into each other at the coffee pot or on the way to a conference room and get into a conversation. An idea results.

Despite its limitations, Figure 3-5 tells us that the likelihood that we will communicate with someone is strongly determined by the distance between us at any time. The distance between workstations is important because that is where people at work spend most of their time. If the distance between workstations is great and communication is desirable, then creatively locating other sites that people use will draw their centers of gravity more closely together.

Minimizing the distance between workstations, however, is only one element. Again, people do not spend all of their time at their workstations; rather, they move about in facilities, sometimes working in conference rooms or other locations. The degree to which they share *these* locations with someone is certainly a strong determinant of whether the two people will communicate. Face-to-face communication (other than through videoconferencing) requires being in the same physical space (Monge et al. 1985).[1]

Influencing Centers of Gravity

The idea of influencing people's workday centers of gravity recognizes this fact that people usually work in more than one place in any facility and come into contact in places other than offices. If the desire is to increase communication among any set of people, one way to do so is to influence the probability that they will be in the same place at the same time. This can mean positioning offices or workstations near to or separated from one another, but it also can be accomplished by positioning other spaces that people use in ways that will draw them toward one another. To improve communication between two groups, for instance, facilities or equipment

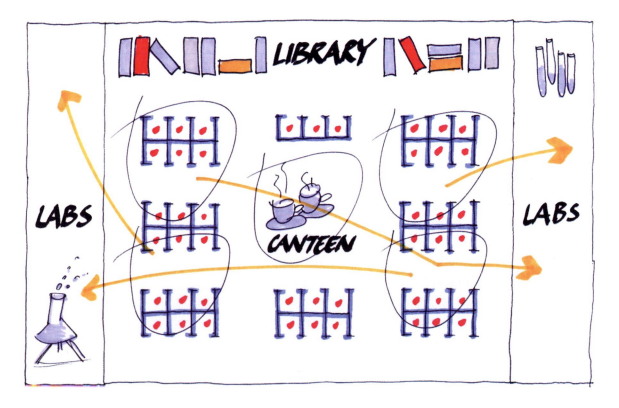

Figure 4-2 The physical space configuration of this small chemical company and the traffic paths the configuration establishes promote communication across departments. The location of the laboratories relative to the offices moves some centers of gravity closer together.

that the groups use frequently could be situated in such a way that members of each group have to walk through the other group's office area to get to the facilities. This is exactly what was done in a small chemical company.

The company had a new facility designed and constructed a few years back. We were able to discuss some of the concepts behind the facility design with management and the architects before the building went up. We also had the opportunity to measure communication before and after the organization moved into the new facility.

The new building housed four departments, arranged in a roughly square pattern around a central dining area/meeting space (Figure 4-2). Laboratories and pilot plant areas were located on either side of the office square, at two ends of the rectangular building. The chemists, engineers, and managers in each department were housed in adjacent offices. The aim of this physical proximity was to promote communication within each department, and it was quite successful in doing so. Still, there was an *inter*departmental communication problem, which was partially resolved by influencing the centers of gravity of the department members.

How were centers of gravity influenced? Space was configured specifically for this purpose. A central canteen/dining area/meeting room sought to draw people toward the center of the building; this was done, in part, by providing coffee all day. Department heads' offices also were centrally located to promote interaction among the managers and to draw their subordinates more to the center of the building. Laboratory assignments were made not on the basis of convenience, with the chemists given labs adjacent to their office clusters, because that would likely have caused further separation among the four departments and reinforced the effect of the separate organizational units and the physically separate office clusters. Rather, because communication among the departments had been so poor, the company decided to create some "functional inconvenience" and assign labs in a way that forced the scientists to travel from office to lab.

Functional Inconvenience

By *functional inconvenience* we mean the introduction in a building of a feature that at first appears to decrease efficiency and make things *less* convenient for occupants but may actually *increase* building effectiveness. The Stata Center at MIT incorporates features that are intended to draw movement along paths that are indirect but that expose the "traveler" to objects and activities they might otherwise never encounter. The hope is that the unexpected encounters may stimulate connections and creativity that might never have occurred.

As the arrows in Figure 4-2 indicate, the scientists had to travel *through* the office areas of departments *other* than their own to move between their labs and their offices. Ideally, a completely criss-cross pattern of laboratory assignments would have been created. This was theoretically possible, since the four departments were located at four corners of a square, and the laboratory areas were located at two of the edges of the same square. However, the constraints of some shared equipment and similar service needs made it unworkable, so the pairs of groups on each side of the building were instead brought together in a shared laboratory space and all four groups used a common test area.

The reconfiguration of physical space at this small chemical company had a strong effect on communication, as we show in Table 4-1.

Managers have two tools at their disposal—organizational structure and physical space—to influence communication and centers of gravity, promote collaboration, and create awareness.

TABLE 4-1 The Effects of Shared Office and Shared Laboratory Space on Communication

Relative Location of Pairs of Chemists	Probability of Weekly Communication
Shared Laboratory/Separate Offices	0.66
Shared Office[*]	0.77

[*] Some with and some without shared laboratory (Tomlin 1977).

Not All Barriers Can Be Overcome with Space Configuration

The vice president of a high-technology company was quite concerned about the lack of communication among his organizational subunits, which were located in several different buildings distributed throughout a metropolitan area. The obvious solution seemed to be to locate all of them together in a single building. We used Netgraphing (detailed in Chapter 3) to confirm his suspicions before he went to the board of directors to get funding for a facility.

Close examination, though, revealed that even some subunits housed in the same buildings did not communicate any more than those that were geographically separated. This was curious, so we went to inspect the building. We expected to find some physical barriers that prevented one group from coming into contact with the other. However, it turned out that the building was no impediment. While these subunits were housed at separate ends, they were on the same floor. What we *did* find was that the subunits had created their own barriers, each sealing off its own territory with temporary walls and filing cabinets and anything else they could find.

We presented our observations at a meeting of the subunit managers, and they were not surprised. The company had long encouraged internal entrepreneurship among these managers—with tremendous success that had made it possible to move into several new market areas with new products. And what are entrepreneurs like, if not independent?[2] They want to run their own "show," like independent businesses. At this company, it meant the subunits were largely ignoring groups that supported advanced technology. Each internal "business" wanted to develop its own technology. The technology groups responded in kind, also turning themselves into entrepreneurial business units as well. The result of all of this was that the overall company had become an assemblage of small, independent "companies" that all largely ignored the resources and synergies potentially available to them through intrafirm interaction. Putting all of these units together in a single building, even a well-designed one, would probably not increase communication. There are some barriers that physical space configuration cannot overcome.

We share this story only to reinforce that using the two management tools of organizational structure and physical space is very complex. There is no simple, magic formula. We know it requires communication and that awareness is a key to the innovation process. Physical space and organizational structure can help or be hindrances.

Skoda Assembly Plant—Awareness of Quality

The Skoda automobile assembly facility, opened in 1996 in Mladá Boleslav, in the Czech Republic, is an example of using space to increase awareness—in this case, of *quality* and *the nature of the actual production process.* This is an example in which the locus of awareness is situated along the assembly line, which is curved around a central spine containing management and administrative offices. Here, people who once were physically separated—and whose knowledge is intimately linked in the design and production processes related to the product—now find themselves not only together in the same space but also in constant visual contact with that process. They are intimately aware of the nature of that process and in contact with events on the production process in *real time.*

What makes the Skoda plant truly unique is the potential for linking components of the automobile assembly, including not only the physical manufacture, but also the design and management of the process and the management of the company as a whole. The task of assembling a car may be clear, but the possibilities for *how* to do it are virtually limitless.

The old linear (or time and motion) principle of assembly line production persisted for a very long time. Products were assembled in single, repetitive operations. Even the innovation process was linear. Designers developed and tested a prototype; plans were then drawn up and sent to a manufacturing facility where workers assembled the product. The individual worker had little, if any, awareness of the number and variety of steps or his specific role in the overall work. This is why it was possible, in the second half of the twentieth century, to replace people on the auto assembly line with "unthinking" robots.

As automobiles grew in complexity, this approach to innovation and production became increasingly obsolete. Group processes became more important. Hierarchical structures were a barrier. Individual workers needed to be more aware of the overall project along with their particular tasks.

The configuration of the Skoda plant (Figure 4-3) allows for greater sharing of information and enhanced awareness. The form of the building follows the flow of the work process and the flow of communication required, which today is based on the fact that cars have many more parts than in the past, including many more electronic components, and are much more complex to assemble. In the Skoda plant, everyone is situated at a level that allows continuous observation of the activities in the auto assembly process and enables on-line problem solving and improved quality of the product.

Figure 4-3 The form of the Skoda plant's interior follows the flow of the assembly process and promotes awareness of what is happening in the process.

Two basic principles influence the design of the Skoda plant. One is the importance of awareness. Managers and engineers are kept aware on a real-time basis of what is happening on the assembly line. They are not sitting in geographically remote offices, imagining that they know what is happening but only discovering problems after significant delay and often with insufficient information. The second principle is that of the *spine.* The spine running through the plant is the locus of activity. All activities beyond the physical assembly take place here. Employees are drawn to this central spine, and this is where information can be exchanged on an informal basis. The evolution of the design is shown in Figure 4-4.

Figure 4-4a depicts the initial design, largely replicating the traditional auto plant. The inner "street" would serve as a logistics service axis, with attached areas serving production. Figure 4-4b shows a further development of the spine concept, with the logistics moved to the outside, thus freeing the center of the "street" for some other

Figure 4-4 The design of the Skoda layout passed through several stages before the physical space, organizational structure, and flow of work were completely integrated.

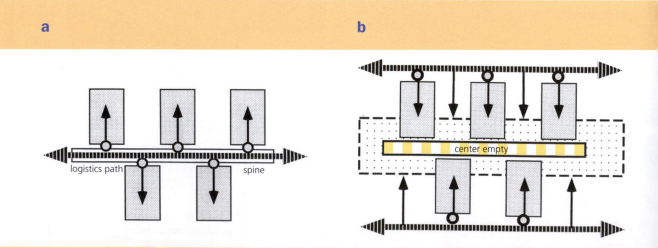

use. In Figure 4-4c, the center, now available, could accommodate production functions. Two kinds of production areas are available: the linear core production and the preassembly areas on both sides.

In Figure 4-4d, which illustrates the ultimate concept for the factory from which the final design was derived, the central production line is closed into a ring. The core production is moved to the two outer areas of the spine. In the spine's center are offices (for the functions of control, processing, logistics, operations scheduling, and human resources management), meeting rooms, team rooms, break areas, quality areas, test space, and a showroom. It is not an office "building" at this center of the spine; there are no permanent partitions between the production line and these offices. The office as an entity in and of itself does not exist; rather, management and the assembly workforce are integrated within the physical space, with visual contact in real time as a constant feature. Figure 4-5 shows the final design of the Skoda factory.

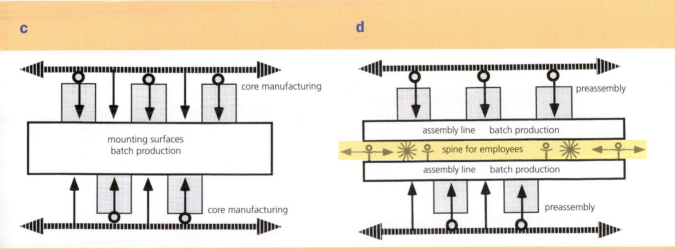

Figure 4-5 The final layout of the Skoda plant shows how the building serves a new approach to the production process.

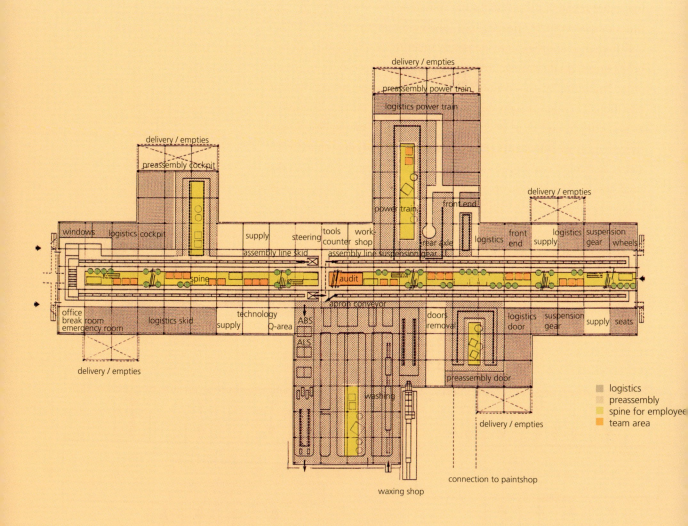

The Skoda plant promotes awareness and communication. Each worker on the assembly line knows much of what is going on within the spine, and the functional managers are constantly aware of the work on the line. Information can be shared in real time throughout the flow of the work process. Integrating the offices in the production line transforms the simple spine in the first iteration (Figure 4-4a) into a communication street where all employees can see that they are working together toward a common objective.

By linking production and office work, barriers are lifted. The value of the proximity of the employees assembling the car and the management responsible is significant. As the production manager has said, "I can be anywhere in this plant in two minutes. I can see everything that goes on. We can begin to solve problems instantly, with the participation of employees at every level." If you were to ask where the plant manager's office is, the answer would be that the *entire* plant is his office. His office is part of the production line and vice versa.

Each person in the Skoda factory is aware of what everyone else is doing and aware of the processes as they unfold. By bringing the office functions and production together, both changed and improved. All the employees know and see what they are working toward. The entrance to the Skoda plant is at the point where finished cars leave the building. *Everyone* who works in the plant must pass by this point to get in and out of the building. This builds awareness. The employees see not only that high-quality cars come out at the end of the day, but they also see everyone's role in the process of producing quality cars clearly.

We find another example of using the two management tools of organizational structure and physical space to promote awareness in a completely different environment—an academic institution.

Technical University of Munich—Awareness of Learning

The building for the Faculty of Mechanical Engineering at the Technical University of Munich (opened in May 1997) is structured like a city—in this case, a knowledge and learning city. Seven institutes of the Faculty of Mechanical Engineering are arranged like houses on a 220-meter long enclosed "street" that defines the spine of the building (Figure 4-6). Learning means exchange, and it is in the spine where students, faculty, and staff have the highest probability of meeting other people and exchanging ideas. This lively, bustling main street is the center of gravity, serving as a traffic thoroughfare as well as the principal space for interaction.

Figure 4-6 The interior "street" of the Technical University of Munich promotes visual contact and awareness and provides space for informal contact.

The spine is a large space that runs the entire length of the building, four stories high with a roof, which promotes visual awareness of all activity within the spine. Just as in a real city, the more public the spaces, the closer they are to the main street. Various shops, places to eat, seminar rooms, and auditoriums are along the spine, and the library and childcare facility are close by (Figure 4-7).

Each institute has a reception and presentation area not "down a side street" but along the main street to draw attention to its work and its disciplinary specialty. These areas attract students to choose their majors. Bridges, galleries, windows, and the transparency of the various levels of the building reinforce visual links between the "network" of institutes. Within the institute "houses" off the street— seven triangular sections of the building—are offices of the institute chairs and other faculty, all situated around open spaces. The least public areas, such as workshops and laboratories, are in sections of the building far from, but parallel to, the spine (Figure 4-8).

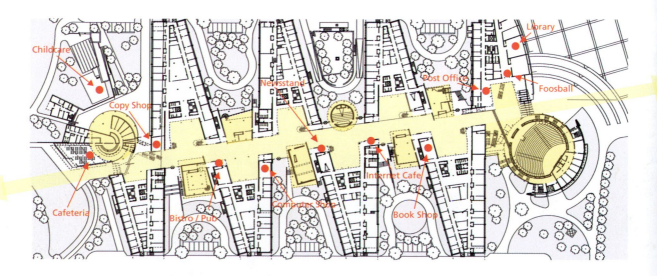

Figure 4-7 The layout of the Technical University of Munich "street" shows how the interior of the building is organized to promote awareness and interaction among students, faculty, and others.

Figure 4-8 Technical University of Munich

The building's physical space configuration corresponds to the requirements of a modern university for *communication* and *concentration* areas. The order, orientation, and room structure correspond to these requirements. The primary space for *communication* is closest to the spine, and promotes dialogue and the exchange of ideas and opinions. The primary space for *concentration*—the work of individual scientists and engineers, or their joint work in laboratories—is in the less public areas. Beyond this, however, the street-like spine, fashioned after an urban street, helps eliminate the typical barriers to communication between students and faculty associated with private offices, secretaries sitting outside, and closed doors. A meeting on the street replicates, to the degree possible within the university building, the kind of informal, chance encounter that might happen were a student and professor to run into each other off campus in, for example, a bookstore.

The evidence that the deliberate physical configuration of the Technical University building accomplishes these objectives comes from Joachim Heinzl, chair of precision engineering and microtechnology in the faculty of Mechanical Engineering. He has, for several years, tracked the numbers of students who choose to matriculate at the university—a number that has grown consistently since the new building opened. While this is in part the result of an overall increase in the number of engineering students throughout Germany, Munich's Mechanical Engineering programs also rose in national rankings during the same period.

In an interview, Professor Heinzl explained that the Technical University of Munich became much more popular with students because of how well communication works, and because of the ideal connections between the faculty's various institutes, which are "very close to each other and connected." Students value the "direct contact" they have with professors and other teaching personnel, and give high marks to the "street"—on which they "meet other students and faculty all the time, and where they can talk and share ideas."

Prior to the physical space configuration being developed, students and faculty were involved in articulating what would work for them in a building. "The layout follows what the people wanted," said the professor.

The Technical University of Munich building is a unique example of using organizational structure and physical space to promote awareness and facilitate communication. The seven institutes form a network to which students have easy access and that builds and makes visual the awareness of learning and the opportunities each institute offers. The physical space establishes equality among the institutes, focusing student and faculty attention on the content of knowledge and scholarship. Further, the physical space configuration supports easy communication for information and coordination and—fulfilling the specific mission established by the faculty—promotes in its main street spine the chance for communication for inspiration.

This building presents us with an example of the spine concept at its best. The spine draws traffic to it and provides space for awareness and interaction. The different spaces that are used by staff and students are situated in a manner that positions centers of gravity along the building's spine. Since all work areas cannot be located in close proximity to one another, the movement of people outside their work areas is used and managed in such a way as to promote interaction among them. In this way, the human limitations shown in Figure 3-6 (Chapter 3) can be overcome.

Interaction and exchange of ideas are the lifeblood of the university. In a building of this size, it would have been easy and likely that groups would become isolated from each other in their private warrens hidden up the side corridors. The openness and attractiveness of the spine draw occupants out of their hideaways and enables them to see others, thus increasing the likelihood of chance encounters and inspirational communication. At the same time, recognizing that academic scholars need private space for concentration and contemplation, the building design follows the example of the monastery—like that in Chapter 1—and provides for that as well.

When we lecture on space allocation for engineers and scientists, managers inevitably ask for our views on the question of open bays versus closed offices. The answer is obvious. Open bays enable communication much better than do closed offices, but they make concentration difficult. Private offices do just the opposite. Since scientists and engineers need space for both of these activities, neither one alone provides the complete answer. The abbots of medieval monasteries knew this and provided space for both concentration and communication. Monks could then use each type of space for its appropriate function.

The same challenge exists in creating space for engineers and scientists, and it is vital to the innovation process. There are many ways of meeting the challenge—as we discuss in Chapter 5.

Notes

[1]   Peter Monge and his colleagues made a compelling argument in several papers that it is not the distance between workstations that determines the likelihood of face-to-face communication but rather what matters is the amount of time people share a specific location (of course, distance between workstations influences the chances that people will be in the same place). They employed a clever means of measuring the amount of time pairs of people shared the same space over several working days, providing each person with a map of the facility and asking them to indicate the amount of time spent in each defined location. Proximity then becomes "…the probability of being in the same 'communication location' during the same interval of time" (Monge and Kirste 1980, p. 112). They found a correlation of 0.47 between this measure and communication. (See also Monge and Eisenberg 1987; Monge et al. 1985.)

[2]   See Roberts (1991) for a thorough study of entrepreneurs, both internal and external, and their characteristics.

References

Allen TJ (1984). *Managing the flow of technology: Technology transfer and the dissemination of technological information within the R&D organization*. Cambridge, MA: MIT Press.

Henn GW (1998). *Form follows flow: Modular plant Skoda Auto a.s.* Munich.

Henn GW (1998). *Technische Universität München, Fakultät für Maschinenwesen Garching: Architektur für eine Stadt des Wissens*. Munich.

Malone TW (2004). *The future of work*. Boston: Harvard Business School Press.

Monge PR, and Eisenberg EM (1987). *Emergent communication networks, handbook of organizational communication*. New York: Sage.

Monge PR, and Kirste KK (1980). Measuring proximity in human organizations. *Social Psychology Quarterly* 43:110–115.

Monge PR, Rothman LW, Eisenberg EM, Miller KI, and Kirste KK (1985). The dynamics of organizational proximity. *Management Science* 31(9):1129–1141.

Roberts EB (1991). *Entrepreneurs in high technology: Lessons from MIT and beyond.* New York: Oxford University Press.

Tomlin B (1977). *Dyadic technical communication in a geographically dispersed research organization.* Cambridge, MA: Massachusetts Institute of Technology, Sloan School of Management.

5 Two Management Tools Employed Together

IN THE PREVIOUS CHAPTERS, we discussed a number of concepts associated with creating the space for innovation. We showed a number of buildings as examples where one or more of these concepts were implemented. Here, in this chapter, the two management tools—organizational structure and physical space—come together in their fullest and most advanced representation. The building featured in this chapter, BMW's Projekthaus, opened in Munich in 2004, is the culmination of nearly two decades' research, discussion, and collaboration between the two authors and key senior managers of BMW on the issue of how these two management tools can be used in tandem and, most effectively, to support the company's innovation process and the specific requirements of product development.

Over the course of the early thinking for the BMW Projekthaus (and for this book), the authors held numerous meetings in Munich, Boston, and Dublin. The Dublin site for meetings was chosen for three reasons: It enabled both authors to escape the immediate demands of their respective organizations; it was convenient to both Boston and Munich; and University College afforded an informal atmosphere to stimulate creative thought. We sought to engage in inspirational communication.

To further this purpose, several of our meetings included senior management representatives from BMW. Our aim was to incorporate the principles described in the preceding chapters into what eventually became the Projekthaus. The assistance of BMW management in this endeavor, particularly Jost Schulte-Wrede, was absolutely essential. He kept us in contact with the realities of managing a very large product development organization.

We reproduce in Figure 5-1 one of his sketches of the BMW product development matrix. It was this sort of vision of what management was trying to accomplish that laid out the problem envelope for us in terms of both organizational structure and physical space needs.

Figure 5-1 In this informal sketch of the BMW matrix organization, which starts with the matrix as depicted in Figure 2-6 (Chapter 2), we see the challenge of ensuring communication between departments and project teams.

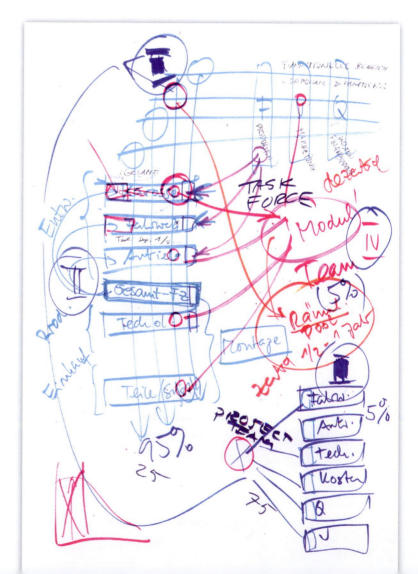

We combined what we learned from managers with our thoughts on the physical space it implied, BMW's need for better communication among product lines, and the need to accommodate the growth and decay of project teams as different developments went through their growth phases asynchronously. One result of our discussion was the Trumpet model of the product development process, first discussed in Chapter 2 and presented again in Figure 5-2.

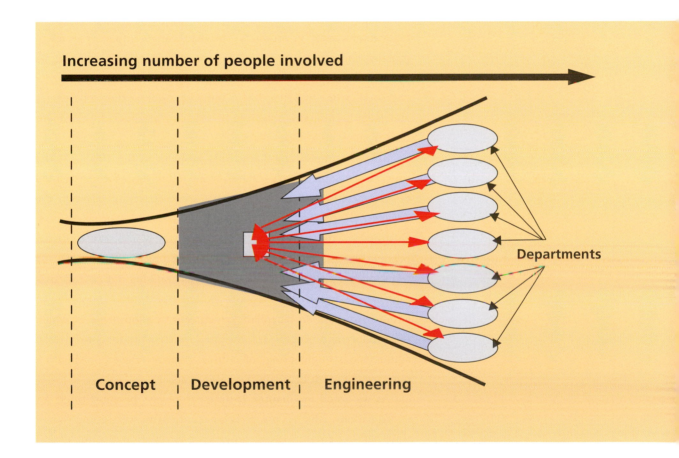

Figure 5-2 The Trumpet model of the product development process shows the expansion of the organization and physical space needs as a development progresses.

The BMW Projekthaus incorporates all of what we now know about the interaction of physical space and organizational structure, and the BMW experience fortifies our belief in the basic principles. But the story of BMW's Projekthaus actually began long before the meetings described above, with a different building—the Research & Innovation Center, located at one of BMW's main sites in Munich. The Center was established in the early 1980s to centralize the research and development process for BMW's automobiles in one location. It was created in response to new technologies, the need for greater variety in products, the increasing complexity of automobiles, and constantly changing process demands. By bringing its product development engineers together with the manufacturing engineers in one building, BMW aimed to address these challenges and meet a company objective of reducing product development time from seven to three years.

BMW's competitors shared this problem in the 1980s. At the time, auto manufacturers—like so many industries—faced extended development time primarily because of a separation between the design of the product and the design of the manufacturing process. Customarily, those responsible for the latter would wait until the product design was nearly complete before designing the process to produce the car. Toyota, however, was cranking out new models much more rapidly. The Toyota example led auto companies to adopt what came to be called "concurrent development," in which the product and process are designed nearly simultaneously. Such simultaneous engineering, of course, requires close coordination between the product and process designers.

As we noted in Chapter 2, time can always be substituted for coordination—which is precisely what auto firms were doing. When time had to be compressed, however, coordination became essential. BMW's senior management determined to solve this problem through an organizational structure that promoted simultaneous engineering and by configuring physical space that made the necessary coordination easier to accomplish. The Research & Innovation Center physical space is configured so that engineers working on the design of a specific BMW product line are in close proximity to, and in close contact with, the people working to fabricate the prototype model as a product is developed. As project teams associated with product lines change, people can easily move so that the matrix is as reconfigurable as is the physical space. For BMW, it was the first time that organizational structure and physical space were employed as equal partners in supporting the product development process.

Over time, as BMW enjoyed the benefits of what the Center offered the company, new demands for an even better product development process emerged. This highlighted some of the limitations of the Center. For example, BMW found that there was very good communication within a given product line such as the 5 Series car, but that people working on that product line were not necessarily aware of the work being done on the 7 Series car. An innovation incorporated into the 5 Series might have been extremely useful for the 7 Series product, but it would be missed or only discovered at a point in the process that was less than optimal (Loch and Terwiesch 1999; Terwiesch et al. 2002). There was insufficient cross-program, cross-product awareness. One reason for this was the vertical separation of project teams located on different floors.

BMW also realized that product development would be enhanced even more if the links between product design engineers and the prototype assemblers were strengthened. In the Research & Innovation Center, their workspaces were situated adjacent to each other. Perhaps they could work in the same space. These were only a few of the considerations brought to bear in BMW's decision to create a Projekthaus that would support BMW's product development process.

The basic idea behind what BMW calls its Product Emerging Process (PEP[1]) concerns the path from idea to manufacturing. Once an idea is generated, the evolving "model" of the car is always at the center. As the development project unfolds, the number of people involved grows greater. In the conceptual phase, people with particular expertise work together centrally in a team. Later, a smaller core team works out problems and issues. All along, communication and informal coordination are key. The crucial changes that the project group must undergo as the development process advances must be as seamless as possible. The transitions from one phase to another in the product development process require special attention and support. In PEP, innovations are seen as the result of interaction between individual activity in the specific workplace and face-to-face communication with other people.

BMW needed a Projekthaus that could accommodate product development interdisciplinary teams of up to 200 engineers and specialists working together, with a configuration of physical space that could ensure that the right people meet at the right time so that development could unfold in real time. This would mean a physical space that would promote communication, knowledge sharing, and awareness. The physical space would need to reflect the creative process for innovation.

The BMW Projekthaus in Munich

The BMW Projekthaus is a convergence of the ideas presented earlier in this book. One is the critical nature of awareness and the necessity of visual contact to create and ensure awareness. A second is the structure for effective product development. Another is the notion of centers of gravity—those that evolve as people move within physical space and those that are created purposefully. Features of a physical space can draw people in certain directions, and the BMW Projekthaus employs such features to influence the centers of gravity. "Coordinating innovation from the center is taken literally at BMW Group," wrote *Business Week* in citing the company as one of the world's most innovative in 2006 (McGregor 2006, p. 67).

Like the Research & Innovation Center, the Projekthaus (Figure 5-3) shows how a physical space can be configured to accommodate a matrix organization. The Projekthaus goes further, however, to show that physical space can be configured *specifically* to make the matrix organizational structure visible to those who work within it. The building is a kind of physical matrix to complement BMW's *organizational* matrix. It is not, however, a static physical representation of an organizational chart; rather, it allows for a dynamic approach to the matrix organization, where change according to what projects need is possible and facilitated by the physical space. In this way, the Projekthaus organizational structure and physical space are part and parcel of an optimized system.

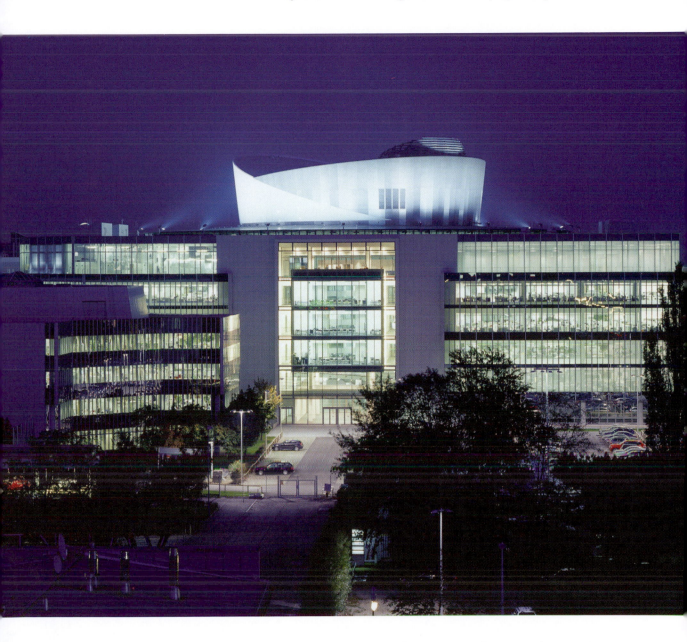

Figure 5-3 In the BMW Projekthaus, departments are located around a center core where most direct project work is done.

Departments are housed in an outer ring and project activities take place in the inner space (Figures 5-4 and 5-5).

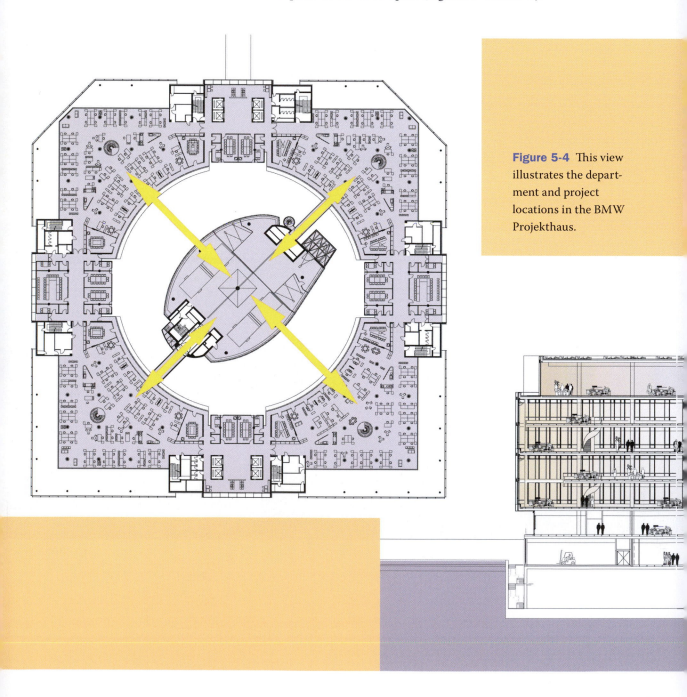

Figure 5-4 This view illustrates the department and project locations in the BMW Projekthaus.

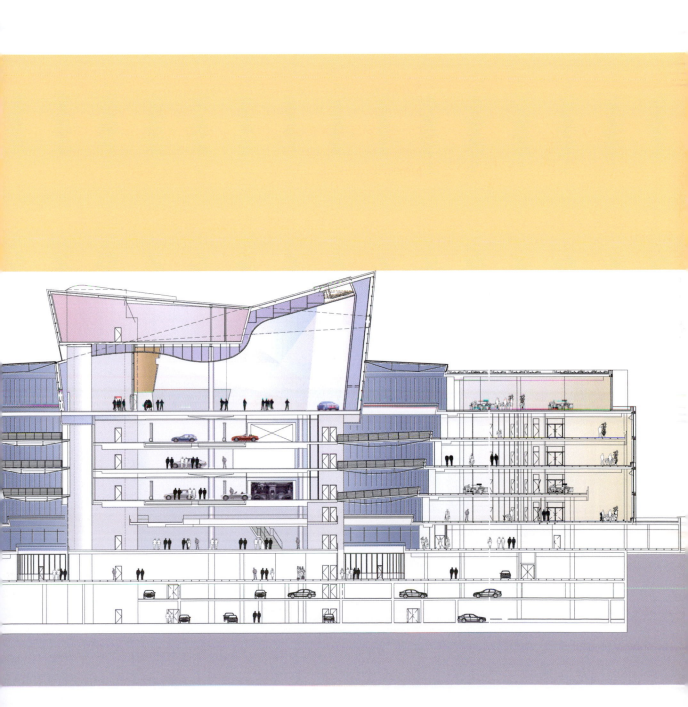

Figure 5-5 The prototype of each car under development is at the center on each floor of the BMW Projekthaus.

There is a constant flow of people back and forth across bridges that link the departmental and project space (Figure 5-6). In the building, it becomes clear as people move in and out of their spatial configurations to do their work that the project, which is visible to all, is the "boss." As *Business Week* wrote, the Projekthaus is a "unique structure that lets [project teams] work a short walk from the company's 8,000 researchers and developers and alongside life-size clay prototypes of the car in development" (McGregor 2006, p. 67). Looking down into the Projekthaus, one sees the matrix physically working.

Figure 5-6 Connecting bridges in the BMW Projekthaus physically link the departmental and project space.

Figure 5-7 shows an example of the open office space on two levels of the Projekthaus. Awareness flows in part from the visual contact with people and products that the physical space enables. There are hardly any borders or barriers between floors. The large atrium allows visibility from floor to floor. In the Projekthaus, you notice what is reminiscent of a beehive of activity within each of the pockets or clusters within the central space that houses the projects. The boss—*the project*—is at the center of the building. In addition, the space is flexible. People and the project teams can move to the optimal workspace. Projects can grow or contract readily, without the need to move walls or reposition lights or ventilation or electrical outlets. The ability to adapt to the changing needs of innovation projects and the changing numbers of people involved makes the building a physical representation of what is required in Phase II of the Trumpet model of the product development process (Figure 5-2).

Figure 5-7 Open office space in the BMW Projekthaus allows for visual contact and ease of communication between people. It can be easily reconfigured according to project needs.

The center open-space area was conceived to be like the *agora* (marketplace) of ancient Athens, where democracy was institutionalized (Figure 5-8). In the Projekthaus, it is a democratic marketplace of *ideas* shared among BMW's engineers working on innovation. In this open space, designers and engineers see each other and see the prototype cars being worked on, in real time. In the middle of the building sits the model of the car. In this case, the spine is a vertical one. Activities are drawn toward it, and the positioning of prototypes vertically along the spine draws attention and contributes to awareness. Engineers must pass the prototype as they enter and leave the building each day. But it is not a static model. From one day to the next, it will be different, because each day's work is added to the model. CAD systems have become so powerful that the design engineer can sit at a workstation for a few hours, accomplish what not long ago would have been unimaginable, and then speak with other designers and engineers about what has been accomplished. People work alone, and then they come together. All can offer their insights, even if it is in an area that is not their discipline. All have the opportunity to learn. The designer of airbags learns from the engineer of transmissions. People are drawn to the model, which is the center of awareness. The relevant vehicle engineers and vehicle specialists regularly meet around the model of, for instance, a front-axle support whenever they have to coordinate work with their colleagues.

Figure 5-8 BMW Projekthaus

The galleries around the Projekthaus central open space house the tools of product development. From the center, everyone has visual contact—vertical and horizontal—that allows awareness of all others working in the building (Figure 5-9). From the mezzanine, people can always see who is above and below. People are drawn to the projects via the bridges they cross to travel to and from work-

Figure 5-9 BMW Projekthaus

spaces. The space supports the informality that allows workers from various disciplines to encounter one another by chance, to share their emotional responses to the work, to be together, face-to-face, to discuss the next steps in their work to design BMW's cars, and to engage in creative and inspiring communication, which is vital to a company's ongoing innovation.

The Projekthaus is a catalyst of creativity for BMW. The physical space and organizational structure the company has established have made BMW's engineers more nimble; they can make decisions more quickly and flexibly. The possibilities for communication of all three types—for coordination, information, and inspiration—the Projekthaus affords help generate new knowledge for BMW's product development process, which now takes less time than before because of the way in which the company has put the two management tools of organizational structure and physical space to work.

Reflecting Back

As we reflect back on what we have sought to communicate in this volume, there are several messages we hope will have come through clearly to the reader.

The first message is that managers, when organizing for innovation, must never forget the organization's physical space and the physical location of those who work in the organization. Innovation results from collaboration and collective intelligence. A successful innovation process requires an organizational structure that makes collaboration and the sharing of knowledge possible. It also requires communication for inspiration that can unfold in real time. A given organizational structure can help meet those requirements only up to a point. Ultimately, the physical space within which people work must also be configured appropriately. As we said in Chapter 1, these two management tools—organizational structure and physical space—are co-equal partners in moving the innovation process forward. To accomplish this mission requires the intelligent combination and use of physical space and organizational structure. Neither by itself is sufficient.

Effective strategies for managing innovation can be derived through systematic empirical research that goes well beyond the observation of "best practice" or isolated case studies. This includes the issue of the appropriate organizational structure for innovation and the product development process, which can be designed on a rational basis as long as several factors are considered. Managers need to be concerned with the rate of change in technology, the degree of interdependence among the elements of the process, the time available and required to bring a product out, and what is happening in the market. These needs can be accommodated through combinations of rationally designed organizational structure and physical layout space configuration that allow for the various types of communication suggested by these needs—including the communication for inspiration that is vital to the complex innovation process.

Success in today's complex innovation process depends upon getting the right information to the right people at the right time. Person-to-person communication networks can accomplish this, but only if the organizational and physical environment enables such networks to develop the appropriate structure.

A corollary to the message for managers above is that architects who create buildings for organizations engaged in innovation must go far beyond their traditional programming process. They need to understand the role of different types of communication and the desired patterns of interaction within their clients' organizations. We've presented some tools in earlier chapters that allow for capturing this sort of information. Architects can play an essential role in arming managers with the *tool* of physical space to help them plan and direct a successful innovation process.

These are but a brief set of the possible conclusions we hope the serious reader will reach in reading this volume. Our principal goal is to influence the thinking of both managers and architects. We hope that we have helped to broaden their consideration when designing organizations and the physical space to be used by organizations. Most important, we hope that our book will play some small part in bringing these two disciplines together—in the context of the innovation process—and that managers and architects will no longer think about the two tools of organizational structure and physical space in isolation, one from the other.

Note

[1]   *Produkt EntstehungsProzess.*

References

Henn GW (2004). *Das Projekthaus: Die Neue Mitte im FIZ*. Hamburg: Junius.

Loch CH, and Terwiesch C (1999). Accelerating the process of engineering change orders: Capacity and congestion effects. *Journal of Product Innovation Management* 16(March):145–159.

McGregor J (2006). The world's most innovative companies. *Business Week*, April 24.

Terwiesch C, Loch CH, and De Meyer A (2002). Exchanging preliminary information in concurrent engineering: Alternative coordination strategies. *Organization Science* 13 (4):402–419.

References

Allen TJ (1984). *Managing the flow of technology: Technology transfer and the dissemination of technological information within the R&D organization.* Cambridge, MA: MIT Press.

Allen TJ (1986). Organizational structure, information technology and R&D productivity. *IEEE Transactions on Engineering Management* 33(4): 212–217.

Allen TJ, and Hauptman O (1989). The influence of communication technologies on organization structure: A framework for future research. *Communication Research* 14(5):575–587.

Becker F (1990). *The total workplace: Facilities management and the elastic organization.* New York: Van Nostrand Reinhold.

Biksen JD, and Eveland TK (1986). *New office technology: Planning for people.* New York: Pergamon Press.

Eppinger SD, Whitney DE, Smith RP, and Gebala DA (1994). A model-based method for organizing tasks in product development. *Research in Engineering Design* 6:1–13.

Henn GW (1998). *Form follows flow: Modular plant Skoda Auto a.s.* Munich.

Henn GW (1998). *Technische Universität München, Fakultät für Maschinenwesen Garching: Architektur für eine Stadt des Wissens.* Munich.

Henn GW (2004). *Das Projekthaus: Die Neue Mitte im FIZ.* Hamburg: Junius.

Katz R, and Allen TJ (1982). Investigating the Not Invented Here (NIH) syndrome: A look at the performance, tenure and communication patterns of 50 R&D project groups. *R&D Management* 12(1):7–19.

Loch CH, and Terwiesch C (1999). Accelerating the process of engineering change orders: Capacity and congestion effects. *Journal of Product Innovation Management* 16(March):145–159.

Malone TW (2004). *The future of work.* Boston: Harvard Business School Press.

McGregor J (2006). The world's most innovative companies. *Business Week,* April 24.

Monge PR, and Eisenberg EM (1987). *Emergent communication networks, handbook of organizational communication.* New York: Sage.

Monge PR, and Kirste KK (1980). Measuring proximity in human organizations. *Social Psychology Quarterly* 43:110–115.

Monge PR, Rothman LW, Eisenberg EM, Miller KI, and Kirste KK (1985). The dynamics of organizational proximity. *Management Science* 31(9):1129–1141.

Pelz D, and Andrews F, eds. (1966). *Scientists in organizations: Productive climates for research and development.* New York: Wiley.

Roberts EB (1991). *Entrepreneurs in high technology: Lessons from MIT and beyond.* New York: Oxford University Press.

Schrader S (1996). Die Planbarkeit von Innovationen. *Henn Akademie Proceedings* 1, January 24, 1996.

Schumpeter JA (1934). *The theory of economic development.* Cambridge, MA: Harvard University Press. (First published in German in 1911.)

Terwiesch C, Loch CH, and De Meyer A (2002). Exchanging preliminary information in concurrent engineering: Alternative coordination strategies. *Organization Science* 13(4):402–419.

Tomlin B (1977). *Dyadic technical communication in a geographically dispersed research organization.* Cambridge, MA: Massachusetts Institute of Technology, Sloan School of Management.

Utterback JM (1974). Innovation in industry and the diffusion of technology. *Science* 183:620–626.

Index

Entries marked with fig, tab, or n, indicate a figure, table, or endnote on that page, respectively. Entries marked with ff. indicate the beginning of a long discussion on the topic.